# Impossible Witnesses

Truth,
Abolitionism,
and Slave
Testimony

# Impossible
# Witnesses

Dwight A. McBride

New York University Press • New York and London

NEW YORK UNIVERSITY PRESS
New York and London

© 2001 by New York University

Library of Congress Cataloging-in-Publication Data
McBride, Dwight A.
Impossible witnesses : truth, abolitionism, and slave testimony /
Dwight A. McBride.
p.   cm.
Includes biblographical references (p.   ) and index.
ISBN 0-8147-5604-2 (cloth : alk. paper) —
ISBN 0-8147-5605-0 (pbk. : alk. paper)
1. American prose literature—African American authors—History
and criticism. 2. Antislavery movements—United States—History—
19th century. 3. American prose literature—19th century—History
and criticism. 4. Slaves—United States—Biography—History and
criticism. 5. African Americans—Biography—History and criticism.
6. Slaves' writings, American—History and criticism. 7. Autobiography—
African American authors. 8. Slavery in literature.   I. Title.
PS366.A35 M38 2001
306.3'62'0973—dc21          2001003176

New York University Press books are printed on acid-free paper,
and their binding materials are chosen for strength and durability.

Manufactured in the United States of America
10 9 8 7 6 5 4 3 2 1

*For my parents,*
*James W. McBride, Jr., and Bettye Jean McBride*

The only authentic witness is the one who could not bear witness for what she has seen, the impossible witness.

—Jacques Derrida

Il est de tous les temps le goût de l'homme pour 'l'ailleurs'. Mais l'apparition de la photographie a exaspéré la quête de ce qui est autre: de ses voyages en pays lointains, l'aventurier rapporte, des images qui témoignent de la 'différence'. Cet ailleurs, il le fixe avec la rigueur obstinée de l'ethnologue, la naïveté éblouie des premiers conquérants, ou l'art consommé des premiers plasticiens. Simple constat: aller au bout du monde, c'est aller au bout de soi.    —*Étranges Étrangers: Photographie et Exotisme, 1850/1910*

Black people need witnesses.                              —James Baldwin

# CONTENTS

Acknowledgments    xi

1    Introduction: Bearing Witness: Memory, Theatricality,
     the Body, and Slave Testimony    1

2    Abolitionist Discourse: A Transatlantic Context    16
     Abolitionist Discourse and Romanticism    21
     Reflections on Abolitionist Discourse in England    25
         African Humanity and the Possibility of Rage in Edgeworth,
         Cowper, and Opie    42
         On Whiteness and Humanity: The Example of Blake's
         "The Little Black Boy"    59
     Reflections on Abolitionist Discourse in the U.S.    62
         Emerson and the Fugitive Slave Law: Toward a Theory
         of Whiteness    67
         Troping the Slave: Margaret Fuller's Review of Douglass's
         *Narrative*    75
         The Body as Evidence: Garrison's Defense of David
         Walker's *Appeal*    78

3    "I Know What a Slave Knows": Mary Prince as Witness, or
     the Rhetorical Uses of Experience    85

4    Appropriating the Word: Phillis Wheatley, Religious
     Rhetoric, and the Poetics of Liberation    103

5    Speaking as "the African": Olaudah Equiano's Moral
     Argument against Slavery    120

6    Consider the Audience: Witnessing to the Discursive
     Reader in Douglass's *Narrative*    151

     Afterword    173

     Notes    177
     Bibliography    191
     Index    201
     About the Author    207

# ACKNOWLEDGMENTS

Authors of scholarly endeavors inevitably incur many debts during the production of their work. *Impossible Witnesses: Truth, Abolitionism, and Slave Testimony* certainly represents no exception in this regard. I thank the staffs of the British Library in London, the Huntington Library in Pasadena, UCLA Research Library and Special Collections, the American Library in Paris, and the library at the Centre Georges Pompidou in Paris.

This book would never have been possible without the support, advice, and encouragement of many people who proved in so many ways that they believed in me. For all their help, time, understanding, kindness, and for providing me with a real intellectual community, especially during the years it took to produce the dissertation that preceded this book, I thank the following teachers, friends, and colleagues: Thomas Augst, Lindon Barrett, Juan Battle, Michael Bennett, David Blackmore, Jennifer DeVere Brody, Fred Burwick, Chris Cunningham, Darrell D. Darrisaw, Georgina Dodge, Bill Handley, Phil Harper, Sharon Holland, Jonathan Holloway, Patrick Johnson, Rachel Lee, Arthur Little, Shelia Lloyd, Elizabeth McHenry, John Nieto-Phillips, Cyrus Patell, Jonathan Post, Robert Reid-Pharr, Charles Rowell, Darieck Scott, Jeffrey Shoulson, Eric J. Sundquist, Sam Weber, Michelle M. Wright, Julian Yates; the entire administrative staff of the UCLA English Department, especially Nora Elias, Rick Fagin, Jeanette Gilkison, David Rahmel, and Doris Wang; and a very special thanks to Toni Crowe and Michelle Harding. For their very special friendship and support not only of this project but of my intellectual, spiritual, and emotional well-being in all my endeavors, I thank dear friends Andrew Dechet, Ken Dorfman, Martin Dupuis, Frank Geraci, Fred Haug, Karen Lang, Olivier Lessmann, Olivier Leymarie, Jay Louser and Allen Neilsen, Bob E. Myers, and Lisa B. Thompson. In fact, so much of this book, especially in its early stages as a dissertation, was discussed, debated, and clarified with Bob Myers that it would not have been nearly as interesting or rigorous a process without his input.

Let me also thank the following institutions that have supported and sustained me during my time in graduate school: the Ford Foundation, the University of California Office of the President, the UCLA English Department, and the UCLA Graduate Division. Special thanks are due to Jennifer DeVere Brody, Mark Canuel, Jennifer Fleischner, and Jonathan Holloway for reading and commenting on the manuscript in its final draft stages before publication. Where I have taken their criticism, the book has been made better for it.

I owe a great debt of gratitude to my sister and brother-in-law, Makelia McBride-Hampton and Willie Hampton, for their love and support, which have always been unfailing. And to my parents, James and Bettye McBride, to whom this book is dedicated, my debt cannot be repaid. I also want to express my love and appreciation to Jason K. Martin for aiding and supporting me in the final preparation stages of this book. He is becoming a true partner in all things in my life.

A good part of this book was drafted while I was in residence in the Department of English at Louisiana State University as the Distinguished Dissertation Fellow and Visiting Lecturer. My debts there are also numerous. I thank the following people of the LSU community for their support, friendship, and collegiality: Lynn Berry, Gail Carrithers, the late Matthew Clark, Bainard Cowan, Jesse Gellrich, Michelle Gellrich, Michael Griffith, Rob Hale, Jerry Kennedy, Ricardo Matthews, Preselfannie McDaniels, Ladrica Menson, Elsie Michie, Rick Moreland, James Olney, Laura Sams, Keith Sandiford, Maria Smith, Maria Adams Smith, Leonard and Lisa Vraniak, and the LSU English Department staff, especially Susan Kohler, the late Claudia Scott, and Jennifer Whalen. A special thanks to the students in my senior/graduate seminar, "Abolitionist Discourse," for eagerly and enthusiastically pushing the limits of my thinking about many of the questions involved in this book. I offer a very special thanks to Chris Kisling, Pat and Joan McGee, Jean and Kelly Rahier, and Jesse Wiseman for their freely given friendship and intellectual camaraderie, and for enduring me in the various emotional states precipitated by this work in its early stages. My productivity would not have been nearly so high were it not for Pat McGee's generosity with his comments, conversation, and good food at his table. He made my time at LSU both rewarding and extremely meaningful. He is a model senior colleague.

I also thank the people and institutions that have sustained me in the completion of this work since graduate school: the UC Office of the President, for a year of postdoctoral study; the UCLA English Department, for hosting me, and Eric Sundquist, for being a superb mentor during that postdoctoral year; the National Endowment for the Humanities, for a summer stipend; Raymond Paredes, UCLA associate vice-chancellor for Academic Development, for providing funds for research assistance; the University of Pittsburgh Department of English, for being a wonderful institutional home and for research and travel support; the University of Pittsburgh Office of the Dean of the Faculty of Arts and Sciences, for summer stipend support, leave time, and travel and research support; Jack Daniel, vice-provost at University of Pittsburgh, for providing funds for research assistance; the Mellon Postdoctoral Research Fellowship at the Newberry Library in Chicago, for a crucial year of postdoctoral work during which I benefited from the friendship and conversation of Canon Schmitt, Pat Crain, Diana Robin, and Jim Williams; and the University of Illinois at Chicago's former English Department head, Don Marshall, and the dean of Liberal Arts and Sciences, Stanley Fish, for a semester of leave time.

The bulk of this work was undertaken while I was on faculty at the University of Pittsburgh in the Department of English. Many thanks to all my colleagues there who provided such an intellectually fecund and collegial community in which to work. Among them I especially thank the following for their time, friendship, and support: Jonathan Arac, David Bartholomae (my department chair), Brenda Berrian, Paul Bové, Fiona Cheong, Eric Clarke, Toi Derricotte, Lynn Emmanuel, Jane Feuer, Catherine Gammon, Nancy Glazener, Ronald Judy, the late Carol Kay, Marcia Landy, Colin MacCabe, Donald Petesch, Shalani Puri, and Richard Tobias. The staff of the University of Pittsburgh's English Department was also extraordinary and unflagging in its support. Many thanks to Sue Borello, Maria Cedeno, Peg Chalus, Gerri England, Annette Galluze, Pat Renkiewicz, Sandy Russo, and Connie Sowinski.

This book has been completed since I joined the faculty at the University of Illinois at Chicago (UIC). Even in the short time I have been there, I have friends and colleagues who have supported me and my work a great deal. Among them I thank Thomas Bestual, Nicholas Brown, Mark Canuel, Nancy Cirillo, Jamie Daniel, Lisa Freeman, Judith K. Gardiner, Robin Grey, James Hall, Thomas Hall, Patricia Harkin, Darnell Hawkins, Jamie Hovey, Clark Hulse, John Huntington, Michael Lieb, Chris Messenger, Sterling Plumpp, Barbara Ransby, Mary Beth Rose, Philip Royster, Dave Schaafsma, James Sosnoski, Joseph Tabbi, Ken Warren, Virginia Wright Wexman, and all the graduate student and faculty colleagues from Chicago-area campuses who participate in the UIC Race and Ethnicity Study Group meetings.

I am also deeply grateful to my editor at NYU Press, Eric Zinner. His support and guidance have been unfailing and always timely. To my mind, he exemplifies everything one wants in an editor.

I want also to mention the institutions and departments who have given me a forum in which to present and discuss this work.

I am grateful to the English, literature, and African American studies faculty and graduate students at the following places who shared so generously their thoughts and suggestions about this project: Oberlin College; University of California, San Diego; Loyola University, Chicago; University of Pittsburgh; Miami University; New York University; Ohio State University; University College, Dublin; Trinity College, Dublin; University of California, Irvine; University of Illinois at Chicago; and a host of conferences too numerous to list here in detail. Such opportunities have been priceless in my efforts to clarify the issues involved in this book. Neina Chambers of UCLA, Jeffrey W. Hole of the University of Pittsburgh, and Justin Joyce of UIC were all very able research assistants in this process. I am grateful to each of them.

A deep and heartfelt thank-you goes to the members of my UCLA dissertation committee—Valerie Smith, Emily Apter, and Barbara Packer—for their support not only of the dissertation but of me and of this work at every stage of its development. They have set a standard for the kind of environment and encouragement for learning and intellectual exploration for students that I hope to live up to as a faculty member.

I owe the highest debt of gratitude to my patient and very able dissertation director, Anne K. Mellor. Her expert and detailed readings of the dissertation were always extremely helpful. Without her pointing the way through the numerous texts that make this such a rich and rewarding field of inquiry, this project would have been far more daunting than it was and much less fruitful than it has been. My regard and admiration for her intellect and humanity have only increased throughout the production of this book. She may never know just how much knowing that she believed in me and in my ability to do this work contributed to its completion.

Last, I thank the first person who encouraged me to apply to graduate school at UCLA, recruited me once I had been admitted, routinely checked in with me during my first couple of years there, and always had time to provide some avuncular advice—both solicited and unsolicited. I owe a great deal of thanks to the late Daniel Calder for his intellect, generosity, and support. I wish he could be here to witness the completion of this project.

*Paris, France*
*August 10, 2000*

# 1. INTRODUCTION

## Bearing Witness: Memory, Theatricality, the Body, and Slave Testimony

The chief concern of this book is mapping the rhetorical markers that constitute the terrain of abolitionist discourse. Recasting the abolition debate in terms of a discourse usefully places central significance on the issues of language, rhetorical strategy, audience, and the status and/or production of the "truth" about slavery. This recasting also broadens our considerations of abolitionist discourse to include not just anti-slavery writing but the various discursive forces that gave rise to and made possible, even necessary, such writing. This, in turn, provides a fertile ground on which further and ultimately more probing work in this area is possible. Additionally, this shift in focus has the effect of deepening our understanding of the transatlantic and cosmopolitan quality of abolitionist discourse, thereby complicating much of reigning historiographical wisdom, which historicizes abolitionism in narrow and often nationally delineated contexts.

The primary site of contestation for slavery debates in the nineteenth century was African humanity. Theories such as Hegel's description of Africa in *The Philosophy of History* as the "Unhistorical, Undeveloped Spirit" or "merely isolated sensual existence" and the popular climatological theories disseminated throughout the eighteenth century, along with the obsession of

nineteenth-century anthropologists (fueled by the theory of evolution) with the measurement of race differences,[1] are examples
of racial thinking that circulated widely in an effort to prove that
Africans were fundamentally inferior to Europeans and were,
therefore, especially fitted for slavery. Such ideas also served as
moral justification for much of the treatment of Africans under
slavery. From the content and rhetoric of the debates waged between the anti-slavery agitators and the pro-slavers, one can see
that the major debates were not only over the nature of slavery as
an institution but also over the nature of the slave. Indeed, these
debates reveal much about the moral stakes involved for the slave
master as well. It was Montesquieu who said, with irony: "It is impossible for us to assume that these people [Africans] are men
because if we assumed they were men one would begin to believe
that we ourselves were not Christians" (250).

A preliminary understanding of the issues involved in the
debates over slavery, then, provides a point of departure from
which to explain the discourses that animate, as well as the context that both enables and limits, the testimony of slave narrators.
Such an understanding further uncovers the complex relationship between the slave witness and those who would receive his
or her testimony. The "reader" is not only constructed *by* the witness, but the imagined reader becomes completely discursive *for*
the witness. The reader represents the fray of discourses, so to
speak, into which the witness must enter to be heard at all. This,
as we shall see, has far-reaching implications for slave testimony.[2]

My selection of the variety of texts discussed in this introduction and throughout this book has much to do with the variety of
genres that anti-slavery argument itself assumed. The range included literary texts, political pamphlets, speeches, essays, newspaper articles, historical and scholarly treatises on both the institution and the morality of slavery, and, of course, slave narratives.
This broad-ranging approach to understanding abolitionism,

rather than assuming a hierarchy among these forms, is concerned with the production of meaning that is possible when one considers the interplay of these forms taken together in the terrain that is abolitionist discourse. Rather than observing generic and disciplinary boundaries, my approach requires a break with such observances in order to think more clearly about the narrative and rhetorical strategies and the figurative and philosophical language that create the discursive regularities of abolitionist discourse.

I employ the metaphor of a "discursive terrain" to describe what is created by abolitionist discourse or the abolitionist debates. For the moment, I examine this metaphor of the discursive terrain in order to understand the situation of discourse into which the slave narrator enters when he or she takes pen in hand. If there is a discursive terrain created by abolitionist discourse, what exactly is the function of that terrain? What does that terrain do to the slave narrator? What does it mean to the slave narrator? If the situation of the discursive terrain is that there is a language about slavery that preexists the slave's telling of his or her own experience of slavery, or an entire dialogue or series of debates that preexist the telling of the slave narrator's particular experience, how does one negotiate the terms of slavery in order to be able to tell one's own story? The importance of this idea is that the discursive terrain does not simply function to create a kind of overdetermined way of telling an experience; it creates the very codes through which those who would be readers of the slave narrative understand the experience of slavery. If language enable articulations, language also enables us to read, to decipher, and to interpret those articulations. As a result, it becomes very important for the slave narrator to be able to speak the codes, to speak the language that preexists the telling of his or her story. Hence the story has to conform to certain codes, certain specifications that are overdetermined by the very discursive terrain into which the slave narrator is entering or inserting him- or herself. The variety of examples to follow suggests the extent to which the concerns of abolitionism, almost from the very beginning of its institutionalization (marked by the organizations in Britain, France, and the United States that first appeared in the late eighteenth century to address the problem of slavery), were transatlantic and transgeneric. Considered in this light, a far more cosmopolitan context for abolitionism emerges than that for which reigning scholarship seems to allow.

Related to this situation of the slave narrator with regard to the discursive terrain is Michel Foucault's discussion of the position of the madman in "The Discourse on Language."[3] The slave is also in the position of Foucault's madman with regard to how the madman's language is read and deciphered:

> We have only to think of the systems by which we decipher this speech; we have only to think of the network of institutions established to permit doctors and psychoanalysts to listen to the mad and, at the same time, enabling the mad to come and speak, or, in desperation, to withhold their meager words; we have only to bear all this in mind to suspect that the old division [between *raison* and *folie*] is just as active as ever, even if it is proceeding along different lines and, via new institutions, producing rather different effects. (217)

This relates to the staging of slavery at the auction block and the use of corporal punishment.[4] This is also not unlike the staging of abolitionism, the carting out of black bodies onto the stage to bear witness to their authentic experiences of slavery. It was, after all, common for the slave narrators to deliver their testimonies orally on the abolitionist "lecture circuit" before the accounts were committed to paper and published as narratives. This black body that testified on stage was somehow more truthful than the word of white abolitionists, who were mere witnesses one step re-moved, as they were not themselves slaves. Even eyewitness ac-counts on the part of white abolitionists did not make them au-thentic in this regard—not authentic in the way abolitionists wanted, needed, and desired to have "real" black bodies on stage telling their "real," "authentic" stories.[5]

But let us return to the issue of the overdeterminacy of the slave's testimony. We see that slave testimonies are being framed all the time by the context of their presentation. It is the theater of abolitionism that enables the moment of articulation, the mo-ment of bearing witness. Yet, even as the discursive terrain en-ables these articulations, it also restricts them. Again, as Foucault says, "we only have to think of the network of institutions estab-lished to permit doctors and psychoanalysts to listen to the mad and, at the same time, enabling the mad to come and speak" (217). Abolitionists or potential abolitionists who would hear these testimonies also had to be competent to read abolitionist discourse and had to understand something of the development and dissemination of that discourse in order to be able to hear the slave or the ex-slave. Even more radically, the discourse is what allowed the slave to come and speak in the first place. But to speak of what? It allowed for speech on one's very experience as a slave. That is, it produced the occasion for bearing witness, but to an experience that had already been theorized and proph-esied. In this way, the slave serves as a kind of fulfillment of the prophecy of abolitionist discourse. The slave is the "real" body, the "real" evidence, the "real" fulfillment of what has been told before. Before the slave ever speaks, we know the slave; we know what his or her experience is, and we know how to read that ex-perience. Although we do not ourselves have that experience, we nevertheless know it and recognize it by its language. This is be-cause the language that the slave has to speak in, finally, is the language that will have political efficacy. And the language that will have the greatest degree of efficacy is the language of slavery that the reader already recognizes—the very discourse that creates the situation for the slave to be able to speak to us at all. I mean this both in the theatrical sense of speaking publicly[6] and in the written sense of the slave narratives that we still have today (in terms of the rhetorical performativity of those narratives). In this way, the slave's narrative also bears witness to the accuracy of the reports and testimony of white abolitionists.

In addressing the issue of truth or authenticity in testimony, Foucault offers the following comments:

> Finally, I believe that this will to knowledge, thus reliant upon institutional support and distribution, tends to exercise a sort of pressure, a power of constraint upon other forms of discourse—I am speaking of our own society. I am thinking of the way Western literature has, for centuries, sought to base itself in nature, in the plausible, upon sincerity and science—in short, upon true discourse. (219)

This is instructive when one thinks of the Romantic project of treating or thematizing the common man, the oppressed, and the lowly all as extensions of "Nature." For the Romantics, there was not a more definitive sign of the "authentic" or real than that of Nature. In the context of the idea of theatricality, the slave represents a state of nature. We will have occasion to observe this idea at work in chapter 2, in William Lloyd Garrison's statement about the naturalness of the African's language that David Walker's appeal trades on. The slave is the material—the real, raw material—of abolitionist discourse. The slave is the referent, the point, the very body around which abolitionist discourse coheres and quite literally "makes sense." As is the case with the producers of any narrative, slave witnesses had to understand clearly the terms of the discursive terrain to which they addressed themselves. Once they did, they had to determine how best to mold, bend, and shape their narrative testimony within those terms to achieve their political aims. The narrative challenge, then, was to relate one's story in terms that would "make sense" for one's readership (which I understand here less as a group of "real people" than as a complex of discursive concerns).

But what is there to say about this "sense" that abolitionist discourse makes? What underlies and makes possible this sense? What Nietzsche named the "will to power," Foucault, usefully for our purposes, rearticulates in "The Discourse on Language" as the "will to truth":

> True discourse, liberated by the nature of its form from desire and power, is incapable of recognizing the will to truth which pervades it; and the will to truth, having imposed itself upon us for so long, is such that the truth it seeks to reveal cannot fail to mask it. (219)

The question is: What is being masked about the will to truth of abolitionist discourse? If anything is being masked, it is the overdeterminacy that I have been discussing. What is also being masked in that overdeterminacy is the fact that in using the very terms of the institution of slavery to talk about these human beings as "slaves," "Africans," and later "Negroes," one supports and buttresses the idea that the slave, if not subhuman, is certainly not of the same class of people as free Europeans. It suggests that even abolitionists could more than sustain such a contradiction. I examine this further in my discussion of Thomas Jefferson's *Notes on the State of Virginia* in chapter 5 (though I would scarcely call Jefferson an abolitionist) and of Ralph Waldo Emerson in chapter 2. Both were men who were, in one form or another, opposed to the idea of slavery but who nevertheless harbored a belief in the inferiority of the African. This position was not uncommon in the nineteenth century even among some abolitionists, nor was it viewed as the contradiction we might experience it as today.

Of course, one of the main arguments of the pro-slavery advocates for the justification of slavery was that Africans were not of the same variety of humanity as Europeans and were, therefore, fit for slavery. Even Hegel, in *The Philosophy of History*, contends that Africans are better off in slavery, where they have the chance to improve themselves by association with their European masters, than in their atemporal, nonprogressive existence in Africa —the place without change or history for Hegel (98–99). This explains why abolitionists were constantly responding to this claim in their writings by showing examples of the humanity of the African. What is interesting in this light is that, in this political and philosophical debate, one of the seemingly unavoidable occurrences that persists is the equating of humanity with whiteness—a point I return to in my treatment of William Blake and Margaret Fuller in chapter 2. The deployment of the rhetoric of whiteness reminds us of the currency of the rhetorical possibility of shedding epidermal layers. It returns us to a kind of phenomenal question of the body: the black body as the referent, the signifier, the site of contestation, precisely because of how it is used in the racist practices of pro-slavery advocacy and rearticulated in abolitionist texts.

Even as I employ the trope of a discursive terrain, along with its companion metaphor of theater, to get at the problems of witnessing, I also deploy a third trope of "mapping" to talk about what these slave witnesses have to do to the discursive terrain of abolitionism and to the memory of their experiences in order to bear witness and to tell the "truth" about slavery. It is useful to include mapping in this cluster of tropes because it helps us see the conscious nature of our constructions. In this way, we also see the purposefulness of these tropes. When we say, "I am mapping this out," it is because we want to know how to get someplace, how to talk about the structure or morphology that enables whole ideas, whole discourses. We look out on the world that is unformed and want to impose order and form upon it. That is a very godlike desire. This is not to suggest that other cultures do not do this or that pre–European contact cultures did not have "maps." Everyone has landmarks or *lieux de memoire* that tell what is significant in a given terrain: for example, there is the river where my mother was baptized; that is the place where an elder passed on to the next world; there is the house in which I was born. This is interesting in relation to the slave narrative as well, because often the narratives are told through these kinds of landmarks. James Olney, in his often-cited essay "'I Was Born': Slave Narratives, Their Status as Autobiography and as Literature," discusses how memory functions in slave narratives by offering that "memory creates the *significance* of events in discovering the pattern into which those events fall. And such a pattern, in the kind of autobiography where memory rules, will be a teleological one bringing us, in and through narration, as it were by an inevitable process, to the end of all past moments which is the present" (149). Olney reminds us of the importance of maintaining an awareness of the constructed nature of memory. That very constructedness is among the chief constituents of slave narrative testimony that we want to bear in mind in our examination of the narratives in the chapters to follow.

Mary Prince, for example, maps out the landscape of her memory of slavery in her narrative. She does this through witnessing moments from memory. Even Prince's description of when she arrived at the home of her new master, Captain I——, is telling in this way:

> It was night when I reached my new home. The house was large, and built at the bottom of a very high hill; but I could not

see much of it at night. I saw too much of it afterwards. The
stones and the timber were the best things in it; they were not
so hard as the hearts of the owners. (54)

This description is compelling for several reasons, not the least
of which is that it has traces of the Gothic, with its attention to the
large house and the dark, desolate landscape it occupies. At
other moments, Prince speaks of someone being beaten there
and the salt being poured into his wounds. It is as if these events
of torture themselves become metaphorical landmarks that map
the terrain of Prince's memory of slavery—not unlike the fact
that even the house is not allowed to remain only a literal house.
It too, in the landscape of Prince's memory, becomes metaphor,
indeed, is anthropomorphized: "The stones and the timber were
the best things in it; they were not so hard as the hearts of the
owners." Rhetorically, the literal material of the house is the "best
thing in it." It is what the house, like the specific events of torture
that are described by Prince in the narrative, represents that is
central in the landscape of slave memory.[7] These metaphorical
mappings are finally very meaningful in slave testimony as well.

This issue of remembering testimony is also interesting in
terms of the idea of the collective body. That is, while this is literally "the history of Mary Prince," Prince's narrative, like any
number of other slave testimonials, implies the impossibility of
telling an individual tale. The slave body is both singular and collective. This is why entire moments of narrative flourish are spent
in these texts describing the treatment of slaves other than the
narrator. While the other slaves are not the slave who is witnessing in the narrative, they are a part of a collective slave body by
condition.[8] In this way, it is impossible to talk about the self singularly. The slave is a self that is always engaged in a kind of collective corporeal condition that makes it virtually impossible to
speak of the self solely as an individual. This is similar to the ex-

istence of black bodies in the racialization of our own contemporary society. This logic goes far toward explaining why white bodies can signify individuality and why black bodies—with their limited access to the category of the individual—almost always signify as representative bodies. Individual slave experiences of horror, torture, and scarred bodies are not in themselves meaningful. By saying this, I do not mean to deny their importance. Rather, I suggest that these instances are like individualized articulations in relationship to a larger language. They are best understood within a larger context that both sustains them and gives meaning to them. The meaning of these particular events comes through the condition of the collective black body under slavery. Prince's experience literally "makes sense" and has meaning because she locates it in the collective—which includes a variety of other slaves' experiences that witness and legitimate her own. So while we might recognize, in Prince's case, the liberatory and legitimating possibilities in the use of such a collective or representative race discourse, we also see in our own contemporary circumstances the limits it can represent.

Still in this way, Prince's narrative is not unlike the conclusion of Toni Morrison's *Beloved*—a contemporary retelling of the effects of slavery that carefully observes the rhetorical strategies of nineteenth-century discourse about slavery—where the experience of the ghost Beloved in 124 "makes sense" only in the context of the collective community. Only in the communal context can the black women and former slaves understand Beloved for what/who she is and collectively exorcise her. After the exorcism, the narrator reports:

> They forgot her like a bad dream. After they made up their tales, shaped and decorated them, those that saw her that day on the porch quickly and deliberately forgot her. It took longer for those who had spoken to her, lived with her, fallen in love

with her, to forget, until they realized they couldn't remember
or repeat a single thing she said, and began to believe that,
other than what they themselves were thinking, she hadn't said
anything at all. So, in the end, they forgot her too. Remembering seemed unwise. (274)

Equally compelling in this instant is the fact that when the community collectively decides to forget her, Beloved ceases to be.
The ability both to read and to articulate Beloved here is reliant
on communal recognition of the linguistic codes that would be
necessary to name the "disremembered and unaccounted-for"
figure.

Finally, this kind of return to the body, to physicality, seems to
take us back to a place where one can say something about slave
experience that is not just discursive and not just about narration
and representational politics. Even so, the body is only a space of
limited refuge from discourse. One can retreat into the body but
only until one decides to act in the world. Identity is not just
about being in the body but about the body being in the world.
Not only does the slave body in this way signify in the world, but
the world also signifies and re-creates the slave body. What the
body will be, then, is a contingency. In narrative, it is contingent
on the version of the self that is being articulated at any particular moment. That is to say, the identity of the body is context
bound. To fully grasp this idea, we need only consider the examples of slaves speaking in a community of other slaves versus
slaves speaking to and moving in the world of whites.[9]

In an effort to comprehend more fully the complex cognitive
and narrative negotiations involved in telling the "truth" about
slavery, I isolate, purely for the convenience of analysis, particular strategies used by each of the figures I examine in the following chapters. I do not mean to suggest by this method that any
particular approach I discuss is unique to the writer(s) to whom

I ascribe it. Quite the contrary, these strategies circulate in important ways, and most often do so concurrently. While I might emphasize the mobilization of religious or Christian rhetoric in the work of Phillis Wheatley, for example, this should not suggest that she does not participate in rhetorical and oppositional strategies described in other chapters, or that writers in other chapters do not also make use of religious rhetoric. What should be clearly understood is that each of the strategies represents a significant category in the discursive terrain of abolitionism.

Chapter 2 is an overview of hegemonic white abolitionist discourses in the period. It addresses some of the major literary figures and their representations of and views on slavery,[10] outlines the organizing tropes that animate my understanding of abolitionist discourse, discusses the influence of the discourses of natural rights and natural law, and briefly accounts for the philosophical development of the master-slave dialectic and both its contributions and challenges to abolitionist discourse.

It is here, too, that I suggest that the abolitionist debates need to become a more integrated part of critical accounts of canonical Romanticism. I examine the ways in which black writers of the period used and reevaluated literary tropes and elements conventionally associated with Romanticism. The evidence that these readings provide will, I hope, bear out my assertion of the need to recognize further the links between abolitionism and Romanticism.[11]

In chapter 3, I discuss *The History of Mary Prince*. My reading of this text centers primarily on the argument that Prince privileges an epistemology of experience in her narrative testimony. That is, I am interested in Prince's implied claim that real or authoritative knowledge of slavery is available only through actual slave experience. I am further interested in the political and narrative ramifications that arise as a result of this claim. After all, such a bold assertion of the centrality of a black slave woman's subjectivity to any real understanding of slavery not only challenges pro-slavery arguments but even presses the limits of many of the abolitionist arguments against slavery made in chapter 2.

In addition to this narrative, and in keeping with my transatlantic paradigm, I turn my attention in chapter 4 to the poetry of Phillis Wheatley. My interest in this chapter is to examine the circulation and political function of religious rhetoric in Wheatley's work. I examine the ways in which Wheatley makes use of the Christian God as a common denominator between herself and her white reading audience in order to articulate her resistance to slavery. This leads to my consideration in chapter 5 of *The Interesting Narrative of the Life of Olaudah Equiano*, where I am primarily concerned with reading the narrative as Equiano's moral-philosophical argument against slavery. I am particularly interested in the ways in which both Wheatley and Equiano anticipate the moral arguments of the pro-slavers in their oppositional discourses on Christianity, especially in their own characterizations of the Christian God. I pay close attention to the stylistic and tonal differences of their respective discourses in this regard. While both Wheatley and Equiano know and rehearse the Enlightenment discourses on natural rights quite well, Wheatley's resistance is coded in her figurative, poetic language, while Equiano's takes the form of a more explicit moral-philosophical critique in keeping with philosophical idioms and conventions of the day.

Chapter 6 examines the *Narrative* of Frederick Douglass. In my discussion of this slave narrative, undoubtedly the most often analyzed of the genre, I concern myself chiefly with the issue of the construction of "the reader" or the would-be recipient of the slave testimony. That is, instead of looking specifically at how Douglass authenticates his testimony,[12] I examine the way in which his narrative prescribes or imagines the nature of his discursive reader. To this end, I use Mikhail Bakhtin's analysis in "Discourse in the Novel" as a way of framing the theoretical pursuit of this discursive reader—that is, the confluence of discourses that slave testimony had to address in the process of its articulation (abolitionist needs and concerns, pro-slavery arguments, natural rights discourse, religious and moral arguments about slavery, etc.).[13] Through close examination of the rhetorical gestures in which Douglass participates, I hope to profile the construction that he presumes his reader to be.

As even the most cursory review of black literary production during the nineteenth century demonstrates, the primary concerns of these texts are slavery, racial subjugation, abolitionist politics, and liberation. These concerns, I argue, were articulated under very complex discursive conditions. As a result, I am persuaded that continuing to ask questions about how the authors/speakers of these texts "bear witness" in this way to these experiences provides a rich and meaningful way to engage the complexity of the condition of the slave, which continues to inform the condition of African American testimony to this day.

# 2. ABOLITIONIST DISCOURSE

## A Transatlantic Context

Simply stated, the fundamental intellectual question that animates this project is: What does it mean for a slave to bear witness to, or to tell the "truth" about, slavery? Perhaps at first glance a deceptively modest query, the question raises four primary concerns of this book. First, through the analysis of representative white abolitionist writings from the period, it endeavors to provide a fuller, more textured understanding of such discourses. Second, this more complete understanding of white abolitionist and pro-slavery rhetoric enables us to appreciate the ways in which the narrative and rhetorical strategies of black-authored texts of the period are overdetermined by these discourses. Third, in a complex discursive terrain such as that occupied by the slave narrator, or "witness," the status of testimonial "truth" becomes a real consideration. We must contemplate the ways in which this particular discursive situation calls for the production of a "truth" that not only performs a kind of authenticating gesture for the occasion of its telling but also accounts for the myriad complications posed by the commingling of abolitionist expectations with literary expectations and the objections of pro-slavers. And fourth, I examine how these new readings of black-authored texts both fit into and beg a reconsideration of the traditional ways in which literary and intellectual history have structured our understanding of literary production during the nineteenth century. This critical endeavor is one that includes some reassessment of how we think about Romanticism and abolitionism within the traditional bounds of nationally delineated contexts.

Given the most established scholarly work surrounding British and American Romantic literature, it may at first be difficult to imagine what possible links Romanticism might have to racialized discourse. A deafening silence seems to pervade the scholarship of the period on the contributions of Blacks to and the participation of Blacks in the grand, master narratives of the literary genealogy of Romanticism. This statement does not intend to ignore the occasional (though sparse) mention and treatment by critics of certain canonical Romantic figures on issues surrounding slavery, abolitionism, slave revolts, and so forth. Rarely, however, do such treatments provide sustained readings of how these "aberrant" texts are integrated into the body of work by a writer or of where they belong among the larger literary sensibilities and trends of the period. For example, to my knowledge *Emerson's Antislavery Writings* (1995), edited and introduced by Len Gougeon and Joel Myerson, represents the first time that Emerson's writings against slavery have been collected and contextualized in a sustained way. And while a work such as Gates's *Figures in Black* treats how black writers of the latter part of the eighteenth century and the nineteenth century were establishing a literary tradition of their own (all the while responding to white racist assertions about the ineducable nature of the African), it does not address how our understanding of the master narrative of literary history must be remapped in light of their literary production. Even more interesting, and somewhat disturbing, is that one does not have to look very far to discover that the ties between racialized discourse and Romanticism not only exist but are, in fact, quite abundant. This observation is interesting because of the sheer amount of material by and about Blacks in the nineteenth century that is suppressed, enabling these kinds of silences. It is disturbing because scholarly mappings of Romanticism have endured this silence for so long.[1]

Literary Romanticism in England (roughly 1789 to 1832) coincides with the rise of British abolitionism (the Society for the Abolition of the Slave Trade was formed in 1787)[2] and the fierce parliamentary debates over the cessation of England's participation in the international slave trade, which ended in the passage of the Abolition Bill in 1807. This act was followed by the passage of the Emancipation Bill in 1833. In the United States, literary Romanticism (roughly 1836 to 1865)[3] is nearly concurrent with the formation of the American Anti-Slavery Society (1833) and the rise of the Garrisonian variety of abolitionism, culminating in the epic conflict of the Civil War.

In addition to these relationships between the rise of Romanticism and of racialized discourse, another element in the context that gave rise to abolitionist discourse is the circulation of the language of "natural rights" and "natural laws" in the nineteenth century. Robert M. Cover, in *Justice Accused: Antislavery and the Judicial Process,* historicizes the ways in which the judicial and political discourses of the period (particularly the decisions of justices sitting on the bench) were complicitous in the system of slavery. He begins his analysis with a discussion of natural law and natural rights. These discourses, as they came to influence thinkers and decision makers in the nineteenth century, had sources as disparate as Hobbes's *Leviathan,* Montesquieu's *The Spirit of the Laws,* Rousseau's *Discourse on Inequality* and *The Social Contract,* Paine's *Rights of Man,* and Jefferson's *Notes on the State of Virginia,* among others. Concomitant with the rise of natural rights philosophy and rhetoric was the theorizing of the "master-slave dialectic." The dominant articulations of this idea can perhaps most usefully be traced through the philosophy of Hobbes's *Leviathan,* Hegel's *Phenomenology of Spirit,* Marx's *Grundrisse,* and Nietzsche's *Beyond Good and Evil.* Each of these philosophers provides, in turn, a discussion of the relationship between master and slave that we can certainly consider as having influenced, and as having been influenced by, the intellectual and public debates surrounding African slavery in the nineteenth century.

Similarly, since the progenitors of these discourses of natural rights that influenced social and political thought in Britain and the United States came from France (primarily Montesquieu and Rousseau and the other natural rights philosophers), it is important here to acknowledge the role of French slavery and colonialism. It is certainly possible to extend the cosmopolitianism I argue for in abolitionism to the French as well, which I hope to do in a separate study. Such a consideration would examine the French government's official position (in its various manifestations) on the issue of African slavery.

*Le Code Noir,* the document (with preamble and sixty articles) that regulated the lives of *les Noirs* in France and its colonies, was signed into law in 1685 and remained the law of the land until 1848. Louis Sala-Molins, in *Le Code Noir: Ou le calvaire de Canaan* (1987), contextualizes the code and examines the changes it underwent in the eighteenth and early nineteenth centuries. In so doing, he positions this law in relation to the theology and the philosophy that gave rise to it and that brought about its demise in 1848, when *la Convention nationale* declared the following in an article:

> *La Convention nationale déclare que l'esclavage des nègres dans toutes les colonies est aboli. En conséquence, elle décrète que tous les hommes sans distinction de couleur, domiciliés dans les colonies sont citoyens français, et jouiront de tous les droits assurés par la Constitution.*
> (Sala-Molins, 261)

> The national convention declares that Negro slavery in all its
> colonies is abolished. Consequently, the convention decrees
> that all men, without distinction of color, living in the colonies
> are French citizens and enjoy all the rights guaranteed by the
> Constitution.[4]

Sala-Molins also discusses the work of Rousseau and Montesquieu and how it contributed to the changing attitudes about
slavery in the French Enlightenment, which led to the eventual
abolition of the code and of slavery itself. Additionally, it is important to consider the formation of La Societé des Amis des
Noirs in 1788, just a year before the beginning of the French Revolution, and the texts they produced and that were produced
about them.

The support that American intellectuals such as Thomas
Jefferson, Benjamin Franklin, and Thomas Paine offered the
French Revolution is well documented. Jefferson, for example,
spent a good deal of time in France; in fact, he was there in 1787
when the U.S. Constitution was being drafted. He was greatly in-
fluenced not only by Locke's philosophy of knowledge (espe-
cially his *Essay concerning Human Understanding*) but also by the
natural rights philosophies of Montesquieu and Rousseau.
Thomas Paine was involved in revolutionary activity in the
United States, France, and England; in 1775, in London, he met
Franklin, whose letters of introduction allowed him to go to
Philadelphia where he worked as a journalist. Also around 1775,
Paine wrote his attack on U.S. slavery, *African Slavery in America*,[5]
and the anonymously published *Common Sense*, which encour-
aged American colonists to declare independence from Britain.
*Common Sense* was enormously successful in both the United
States and France. Back in London in 1791, Paine joined the
pamphlet war over the French Revolution with his *The Rights of
Man*,[6] written in response to Edmund Burke's conservative *Re-*

*flections on the Revolution in France.* Burke's *Reflections* also occasioned the publication of Mary Wollstonecraft's *Vindication of the Rights of Man.*

This kind of transatlantic intertextuality served as an occasion for political debate between the Americans and the recently defeated British over the rights of man, with Burke and Paine and Wollstonecraft squaring off as representative interlocutors. Such political and intellectual cross-fertilization demonstrates the need to think of the triangular relationship among these three nations—England, the United States, and France—as framing the political and moral-philosophical discourses that ushered in the nineteenth century and influenced what has been traditionally called literary Romanticism. It strikes me that in light of such compelling evidence, scholarship cannot afford to be timorous about pursuing such connections between racialized discourse and the discourses of Romanticism.

## Abolitionist Discourse and Romanticism

While much historical attention has been devoted to abolitionism, and much literary attention has been given to British and U.S. Romanticisms, little attention has been given to thinking the relationship between Romanticism and the rise of racial politics in the nineteenth century.[7] Such a discussion would not merely be limited to considerations of the appearance of traditional Romantic tropes in black-authored texts—for example, the "innocence" of childhood versus the "experience" of slave identity consciousness, the use of sentimentalism, brief appearances of the Gothic, the thematization of "self-reliance," the valorizing of the meek and lowly or the "natural man," and alienation—but would also include some speculation about the rise of Romanticism in light of the political upheavals surrounding the issue of slavery.

Perhaps literary Romanticism (here the rise of the thematization of Nature in opposition to the idea of a more ordered or mechanized civilization, associated with the Enlightenment) is less about escaping the political realities and anxieties of civilization than about choosing in Nature a more uncertain or less determined terrain on which to work out those political anxieties. Perhaps the contemporary issues associated with civilization[8]—most notably the French Revolution and its aftermath, rampant poverty among a growing underclass, and slavery and abolitionism —that so plagued the creative imagination were more easily worked out in the coded poetic language of Nature than in the highly charged and volatile political terms of the public debates of the day. These kinds of cross-cultural readings may offer new ways of understanding and reading Romanticism as well as the Romantics.

In *Romanticism and Gender*, Anne Mellor poses a monumental question to Romanticists. She asks her readers to reconfigure what they have traditionally known as Romanticism by centering women's writings in that period instead of works by men. Mellor instructs us that under this inverted paradigm, new dominant themes emerge and new aesthetic principles become normative. Mellor's inquiry, then, gets to the heart of the ways in which dominant representations of, in this case, literary Romanticism are established and maintained through the consistent privileging of male-authored texts and the suppression of female-authored texts. In such instances, women's literature will consistently come up short in "critical" assessment when measured against critical paradigms established for literature by men—paradigms that have little bearing on the themes, tropes, and politics that characterize female-authored texts of the period.[9]

Similar to Mellor's project, one of the minor questions for me that is always hovering in the background of this study is: What do British and U.S. Romanticisms look like when we privilege the literary production and the concerns of Blacks during these Romantic periods? Still other queries follow: What themes are recurring? What aesthetic principles become established? What relationship do they have to the white, and predominantly male, literary establishment of the period? What relationship do they have to the literature and the political discourse of white women? Such questions prescribe the kind of cross-cultural analysis that I suggested in my brief discussion of Romanticism. They presume, for example, placing these texts in conversation with canonical Romantic authors and their tropes. The description in some black women's slave narratives of the often-contentious relationship between the slave and her mistress calls into question, for example, Wollstonecraft's analogous use of the trope of "slavery" in *Vindication of the Rights of Woman* to describe the condition of white English women.

Since serious treatment of all these concerns is not possible in the scope of the present project, I propose instead to consider some representative black-authored texts—particularly, though not exclusively, slave narratives, since the primary literary genre for Blacks in the nineteenth century is autobiographical writing—for how they address the questions I have been raising thus far. Following the example of Paul Gilroy in *The Black Atlantic: Modernity and Double Consciousness* (1993), I do not want to restrict prematurely my discussion of the lively interplay of transatlantic discourses that converge around abolitionism and slavery. With that attention to transatlantic intertextuality in mind, I willfully participate in the kind of "transatlantic crossing" that Gilroy charts in his text as a way to defend against the retreat into narrow literary nationalisms that have held sway in the academy for so long. Studies that take up their topics and follow them across whatever national boundaries the work calls for are the more interesting ones.

I make this point about crossing national borders not only to suggest the hybridity of slave narratives in the nineteenth century—a point that Henry Louis Gates, Jr., and Charles T. Davis,[10] among others, have compellingly argued—but also to point out further the hybrid nature of the larger discourses of slavery and abolitionism. Jan Nederveen Pieterse, in *White on Black: Images of Africa and Blacks in Western Popular Culture* (1992), suggests, for example, the vast influence that a number of British writers had on the pro-slavery lobby in the United States:

> In the United States pro-slavery arguments were imported from Europe—Edward Long's *History of Jamaica* was reprinted in New York in 1788. Outdated, denigrating ideas about blacks were revived and books republished to supply the planters with arguments. Renowned authors such as Thomas Carlyle, Anthony Trollope, William Makepeace Thackeray, and Charles Dickens acted as the lobby's spokesmen or underwrote its views. Carlyle's *Occasional Discourse on the Nigger Question* (1849), one of the most virulently racist publications to appear in the nineteenth century, was written in this context. (60)

Another factor that bears mentioning here is that many of the commentators on slavery and abolitionism were literate in languages other than their own. Thus, not only was a text such as Claire de Duras's *Ourika*[11] read by an enthusiastic French public (it saw four editions in France in 1824 alone), but as John Fowles (translator of the 1994 English text) informs us, "Goethe wrote to Alexander von Humboldt (who told Duras of the letter) that he had been 'overwhelmed' by the novel" (xxi). Eva Beatrice Dykes reminds us that an 1824 English translation of *Ourika* was "read eagerly by the English public" (114). Such evidence invites us, as students of the period, to understand the complicated ways in which these ostensibly nationally marked discourses bleed into one another more freely than we might at first imagine.

The more of this material one reads, the more one comes to the conclusion that the national boundaries so often adhered to in studies of this literature are actually quite permeable despite the nationalisms that seem to characterize the period. That is, the abolitionists constituted a new kind of transnational identity, drawing what they needed to support their cause from a variety of sources from around the world. The same, too, can be said of the pro-slavery advocacy. In addition, discussions of narrative authenticity in slave testimony require a kind of hegemony of form and content, also across national boundaries, which also suggests a new kind of transnational identity for the "slave" as well.

## Reflections on Abolitionist Discourse in England

The rise of abolitionism in Britain is represented by a complex set of events. The complexity of this ascension is attested to by the countless histories written on the topic over the last twenty-five years. Still, by way of providing a general background to the present study, certain political trends, events, and notable figures should be emphasized.

Three events of the late eighteenth century influenced and/or frustrated the nascent abolitionist movement in England: the *Somerset* case in 1772, the *Zong* case of 1781, and the Revolt at Saint-Domingue in 1791. The first may be briefly described as follows. James Somerset was a black slave from Virginia who was brought to England by his master. While in England, he escaped and was taken up by Granville Sharp. The case was argued before the Court of the King's Bench, with Lord Mansfield presiding. Lord Mansfield's decision included the following statement, which was to have radical ramifications for the future of British slavery and abolitionist activity:

The state of slavery is of such a nature, that it is incapable of
being introduced on any reason, moral or political; but only
positive law, which preserves its force long after the reasons, occasion, and time itself from whence it was created, is erased
from memory: it's so odious, that nothing can be suffered to
support it, but positive law. Whatever inconveniences, therefore, may follow from a decision, I cannot say this case is allowed or approved by the law of England; and therefore the
black must be discharged.[12]

The repercussions of this case in England cannot be overesti-
mated. Not only was Somerset set at liberty, but the ruling also
freed nearly ten thousand other slaves in Britain. Sharp tried
in subsequent attempts to have the ruling in the *Somerset* case
extended to slaves in the colonies. These were all unsuccessful. Sharp learned that British Common Law "did not apply in
those parts of the Empire where slavery was recognized by colonial law."[13]

The case of the *Zong* is a fascinating one, and one in which, coincidentally, Olaudah Equiano was very much involved, as Robert
J. Allison reminds us.[14] The ship *Zong* left an island off the coast
of West Africa in 1781 with 440 slaves. When it reached the
Caribbean some two months later, sixty slaves and seven members of the crew were dead from disease, and many others were
dying. Knowing that he could not sell even the remaining healthy
slaves, the captain made a "business decision" based on the logic
that insurance would pay for drowned slaves but would not pay
for those who died of disease or those who were ill:

He ordered 54 Africans chained together and thrown over-
board. The next day, he ordered 42 more drowned, and 36 on
the third day. Having covered all evidence of illness, the captain sold the rest of the cargo and sailed for England. When he

arrived in Liverpool, the Zong's owners filed an insurance claim for 132 drowned slaves.

The claim might have gone through quietly, but Equiano learned the true story. . . . Equiano quickly alerted Granville Sharp . . . who had brought the *Somerset* case twelve years earlier. (Allison, 11)

The case was brought before the same Lord Mansfield who had ruled in the *Somerset* case, and he declared that the owners of the *Zong* were entitled to collect the insurance money on the 132 slaves their captain had killed. Seizing the power of public opinion on this incident, abolitionists used the newspapers and lecture platforms to gather support for their opposition to the slave trade. After this massacre, Allison reports,

two of the most notable abolitionists who emerged from the Zong massacre were James Ramsey, a former minister in the West Indies, and Thomas Clarkson, a college student at Cambridge. Ramsey's *Essay on the Treatment and Conversion of African Slaves in the Sugar Colonies* (1784) attacked the West Indian planters for their cruelty, and Clarkson's *Essay on the Slavery and Commerce of the Human Species* (1786) included a cross-section drawing of the slave ship Brookes, showing how Africans were loaded into cargo bays. This illustration became one of the most important images of the abolition movement. (11)

The case of the *Zong* provided much fuel for the abolitionist fire. Howard Temperly notes in *British Antislavery* that this largely had to do with the fact that it sensitized the "unsentimental British public" to the horrors of the trade. The public convinced themselves that whatever the horrors of slavery, they could not compare to this. He further demonstrates that, given the state of public opinion at the time, the trade was a much more viable

target for the abolitionist than was slavery itself, which involved
the more sensitive question of property:

> In choosing to concentrate their energies on the slave trade
> rather than on slavery, British abolitionists had been swayed by
> a variety of considerations. To have attacked both simultane-
> ously would have meant demanding more than public opinion
> could be expected to accept. Of the two, the trade was patently
> more vulnerable. . . . Contemporary opinion, moreover, was
> highly sensitive on questions involving private property and es-
> tablished institutions to which categories slavery clearly be-
> longed, whereas regulating trade had long been recognized as
> a function of Parliament. (Temperley, 6)

This move early on to focus on the trade rather than on slavery
itself was informed as much by the abolitionists' readings of
Parliament and the current political climate as by their gaug-
ing of public opinion. This aptly demonstrates that the abolitionists, while often considered bothersome and extreme by
many of their critics (even those sympathetic to their cause),
were in their strategies neither unreflective about nor incon-
siderate of the climate of political and public opinion in which
they were acting.

Finally, the 1791 revolt of Saint-Domingue, led by François Do-
minique Toussaint-L'Ouverture, which resulted in the liberation
from France of what would become Haiti, sent reverberations
throughout the slaveholding societies of Europe and America.
Many of the advocates for slavery used this revolution to argue
that Africans were uncivilized and inhumane. In contrast, some
abolitionists argued that such retaliatory violence was a pre-
dictable consequence of a violent system such as that of slavery.
Nevertheless, abolitionists and their politics were widely blamed
for the uprising, as Temperley reminds us:

When the slaves in Santo Domingo rose in rebellion in August 1791 their action was widely attributed to the subversive activities of abolitionists. British planters prophesied similar uprisings in their own communities, unless agitation was promptly stopped. During the next decade the abolition question was almost forgotten. Between 1797 and 1804 the London Abolition Committee did not hold a single meeting. (5)

What this tells us is that even in its nascence, the abolitionist movement had to be thoroughly in tune with the political climate of the societies in which it was taking action. Abolitionists understood from the beginning how important it would be for their cause to monitor the tide of public opinion and, whenever possible, to direct it to their advantage.

While it is true that what might be called abolitionist sentiment had been around for as long as slavery itself, as an institutionalized movement, abolitionism in England did not get under way before the 1780s. The first abolitionist organization was founded in 1783 by Quakers in London. The standing Meeting for Sufferings,[15] at the urging of its Philadelphia Quaker counterpart, established a Committee on the Slave Trade who, in the summer of 1783, first petitioned Parliament to declare the slave trade illegal (Temperley, 1–2). This was not, however, the first such motion ever to be made in Parliament. In 1776 (coincidentally, the year marking the beginning of the American Revolution), David Hartley[16] "asserted that it was 'contrary to the laws of God and the rights of man'. Though unsuccessful, Hartley's effort prepared the way for subsequent united political action."[17] Still, the Quakers can be said to have provided much of the initial force for what was to become the abolitionist movement in England.

Historians Howard Temperly, Paul Johnson, and Daniel Littlefield,[18] among others, have suggested that the reason Quakers were among the earliest people in America to support the anti-slavery cause in an organized fashion was the resemblance they saw in slavery to their own persecution, like that of the Jews, at the hands of both Protestants and Catholics. The fact that the Quakers' first abolitionist organization was a committee that grew out of their own standing Meeting for Sufferings, designed to address Quaker persecution, is one key to understanding their rather natural process of seeing the relations between African persecution and their own. Still, prior to the mid-1700s many Quakers themselves owned slaves, including that famous champion of liberty William Penn. According to James Clyde Sellman, the two Quakers who had the earliest and perhaps the strongest influence in galvanizing Quaker resources in the fight against slavery were John Woolman and Anthony Benezet (about whom I say more in chapter 5).[19] Woolman was the author of the pamphlet *Some Considerations on the Keeping of Negroes* (1754), one of the earliest American critiques of slavery. Benezet, forced to leave his native France to settle finally in Philadelphia because of religious persecution, devoted his life to the anti-slavery cause. In addition to establishing integrated schools and writing pamphlets against slavery, he became a scholar of Africa, publishing books that represented Africa as a place of culture and civilization like the West.[20] He argued that "the chains of bondage alone were responsible for any failings they [Africans] showed in America" (Littlefield, 111).[21]

While the Quakers were vital both financially and politically to the anti-slavery movement, they were not the only ones involved in these early stages:

Granville Sharp was still active, and younger men such as Thomas Clarkson and William Wilberforce were also beginning to turn their attention to the moral dilemmas which it [slavery] raised. A broadening of the base of antislavery ef-

forts occurred in May 1787 with the formation of the Society
for the Abolition of the Slave Trade, which brought together
the Quaker and non-Quaker elements in the movement.
The committee of this new organization consisted of five of
the six members of the unofficial Quaker committee, three
other Quakers, and three non-Quakers, among them Granville Sharp, who, as doyen of the British movement, became
the Society's first chairman. (Newey, 2–3)

In addition, other historians, following Eric Williams's economic
thesis on slavery in *Capitalism and Slavery*, point out that religion
was not the only factor in the debates over slavery and abolitionism. Economic concerns and class structure were also important.
C. Duncan Rice best states this case:

Slavery was overthrown when its profitability declined and
when the classes who supported it themselves began to lose
strength. This is not the same as saying that abolition was
nothing but a product of changes in economic needs of the
class structure of western Europe. An abolitionist movement
was produced by the interaction between such economic and
social change, and a complex series of intellectual develop-
ments, philosophical, literary and religious. Occasionally the
abolitionists might have an aristocratic ally, much more occasionally a working-class one. But they were overwhelmingly
drawn from the ranks of the solid businessmen of a rapidly
industrializing world, or the lawyers, clergymen and other
professionals who were their servants. There had been little
reason for the traditional groups of pre-industrial society to
query the viability of making slaves of black men and women.
. . . Those who later turned against slavery had been born
into a more modern world in which it was an anomaly. This
was not only because it was cruel . . . but because it now

seemed less efficient. In any case, it was less important to the economies of the European countries.[22]

I mention the economic critique here because, while it may not account fully for the decline of the institution of slavery, it has a powerful allure for many historians of slavery and of the abolitionist movement. And it should be borne in mind that abolitionism was largely a bourgeois movement. That is, the people with the leisure, the intellect, and the access to the various political and social venues through which to execute their moral outrage were largely members of the middle and upper classes. This point is intended neither to denigrate nor to question the sincerity of the contributions of the abolitionists. It is merely meant to specify the class sensibility characteristic of the rhetoric of all but the most radical segments of the movement.[23]

It should also be noted that the anti-slavery movement in England meant different things during the decades of its existence, from the 1780s to the 1830s and beyond. As mentioned above, early abolitionist activism targeted the slave trade instead of slavery itself as the primary evil to be resisted. The logic of such thinking assumed that slavery was an evil institution primarily because of the human horrors and moral degradation associated with it. The argument went that if the ready supply of slaves were halted through the cessation of the Atlantic slave trade, then the value of the slave would be increased, and the planters in the British colonies would be obliged to treat slaves more humanely because they could not replace them through the means provided by the trade. Those associated with this particular arm of the early abolitionist movement were often known as ameliorationists. This does not, however, mean that all the early abolitionists were ameliorationists. Some, from the very beginnings of the movement, favored emancipation—earning for themselves the appellation "emancipationists." But even most of these early emancipationists understood the need for a more graduated public and political approach to the end of slavery. In the decades after the cessation of the slave trade in 1808, however, the anti-slavery movement became increasingly emancipationist. The issues dividing it at this juncture were subtler, having to do with methods of achieving their ends and disputes over the recompense that should be made by the government to the planters at the time of emancipation.

These early debates over slavery were waged both in moral and in economic terms. Planters argued that they needed the ready supply of slave labor in the colonies to ensure that they would be able to provide England with the raw materials it depended on. In addition, if they were to remain competitive with France, Spain, and others in the trading markets, British planters could not be expected to emancipate their slaves and to maintain competitive trading prices unless emancipation were universal and all the nations decided to emancipate their slaves at once. The abolitionists, seizing on the rhetorical strategy of this logic, countered with their own view of what was in the "national interest." They argued, in a moment of rhetorical flourish, that slavery was actually opposed to the national interest. If the slaves were emancipated and liberated, then they would be happier and more productive. By creating out of former slaves a working class of wage earners, England would create a broader consumer base for the consumption of goods in the colonies. While there are perhaps any number of flaws to the economic viability of the abolitionists' argument, accompanied by the tide of public opinion, it did bring about the first major victory for the abolitionist movement in England:

> In 1805 an abolition Bill was narrowly defeated in the Commons. The following year, thanks to the support of the new

Fox-Grenville Ministry and a clever exploitation of the "national interest" case by the abolitionists, a Bill providing for the abolition of the trade to the conquered colonies triumphantly passed both Houses. In 1807 this was superseded by a stronger measure which forbade the carrying of slaves in British vessels and their importation into any British colony. (Temperley, 6)

The passage of this measure represented the first major political victory for the abolitionist movement. And many had a great deal of faith that this would be enough to ameliorate the institution of slavery, perhaps even to the point that it would gradually and inevitably become extinct.

In examining the evolution of abolition in England, a reading of the rhetorical terms in which Parliament debated the issues of the slave trade and slavery is most revealing. Suffice it to say that the terms were not radically different from those of the general planter lobby and the abolitionists. Generally speaking, the House of Lords was more sympathetic to the planters than was the House of Commons. This is apparent in the debates leading up to the anti-importation measure passed in 1807 and in the report of the Parliament's Select Committee on the Extinction of Slavery Throughout the British Dominions that preceded the 1833 emancipation decision. This division of sympathies is further attested in the findings of two Parliamentary committees that were to report on the success and progress of Britain's decision to end slavery and the slave trade not only in England but universally. The committee of the House of Commons sat during 1848–49 (1849 also marks the publication year of Thomas Carlyle's *An Occasional Discourse on the Nigger Question*, and 1848 marked the cessation of slavery by the French government), and the committee of the House of Lords sat during 1849–50. In their assessments of whether Britain's decision to emancipate the slaves and to cease the trade had ameliorated the living condi-

tions of Africans in the colonies and improved the economic productivity of the same, the reports of the two committees were diametrically opposed. Excerpts from the reports and the proceedings that followed were published in London in 1851.[24]

With the slave trade illegal in Britain, the Society for the Abolition of the Slave Trade in 1807 was replaced by the African Institution. This body established three goals for itself: "to see that
the new laws against the slave trade were properly enforced; to
encourage legitimate commerce with Africa; and to persuade
other countries to follow Britain's example by giving up the
trade" (Temperley, 7). The first was readily achieved, as the government had every intention of making good on the action it had
taken on the slave trade. The remaining two goals were not so
simple, however. The group put all its efforts into establishing a
new British colony for former slaves in Sierra Leone. The idea
was to make it into a well-run colony that would serve as a model
for other nearby African nations. The experiment was not to succeed. Limited resources and numerous scandals involving the
governance of the colony both discredited the African Institution and disillusioned its members. With the failure of Sierra
Leone, the African Institution's "interest in Africa declined, and
from 1814 onwards the Institution's attention focused increasingly on the third objective, the suppression of the slave trade
through international agreement" (Temperley, 8).

To its credit, the British government did make many efforts to
negotiate agreements with other European nations that would
suppress the slave trade. The government was highly moti-
vated in this regard, because it knew that if it did not successfully negotiate such suppression agreements with its European
neighbors, Britain would be unable to remain competitive with
them in the trade markets. These efforts were unsuccessful. The
French, Spanish, and Portuguese all agreed that "while the British had seen that their colonies were kept well stocked with slaves

during the war, other nations had not" (Temperley, 8). Therefore, it was only fair that these countries should have an opportunity to make up the difference before withdrawing from the trade. England rejected these arguments and promised generous financial subsidies if the other countries would cooperate. This offer, too, was refused. It became clear that such an agreement would be very difficult to negotiate. This bespeaks the extent to which these countries understood and were committed to the financial benefits of continuing the slave trade, despite arguments being made to the contrary.

In addition to such setbacks, the abolitionists were increasingly becoming aware of mounting evidence to suggest that the cessation of the slave trade was not, in fact, having the desired effect of ameliorating the life conditions of the slaves. Modern-day British historian Barry W. Higman's population study of the British Caribbean shows that the mortality rates of slaves in the British colonies were not significantly impacted by the trade's cessation.[25] Contemporary evidence came to the abolitionists in the form of testimonials from the colonies, reportings in the *Anti-Slavery Monthly Reporter,* and records of court proceedings. Many instances of cruelty came to light in the testimony given before committees of the House of Commons in 1814:[26]

> Accounts of particular cases of mistreatment which filtered back to England showed only too clearly that colonial courts were as reluctant as ever to interfere between masters and slaves and, when they did so, to impose effective punishments upon the former. Comparisons with the United States census records revealed that West Indian Negroes died earlier and produced fewer offspring, proof, so it was claimed, that the British slave system was harsher and that planters were still practicing their old technique of working their charges to death. (Temperley, 9)

The increasing variety of this kind of evidence led in 1823 to the establishment of the Society for the Mitigation and Gradual Abolition of Slavery throughout the British Dominions, or the Anti-Slavery Society. The membership was not very different from that of the African Institution, but its focus was. The society demanded the "adoption of measures to protect slaves from wanton mistreatment, together with a plan for gradual emancipation leading ultimately to complete freedom. By limiting itself to such proposals it sought to enlist the support not only of radicals but of conservatives and even of the planters themselves" (Temperley, 10). Thomas Clarkson went on the road for the group and encouraged the establishment of local auxiliary bodies that would contribute to the work of the larger society. By 1826 the Anti-Slavery Society had seventy-one local chapters throughout England, with Quaker membership and support once again being in great evidence (Temperley, 10).

In the decade after 1823, the work and agitation of abolitionists, especially Thomas Fowell Buxton, caused Parliament to take certain legal actions to improve the lot and condition of the slaves in the colonies. While Parliament did not adopt the strict measures submitted to them by the abolitionists, it did adopt certain diluted versions of these measures that it passed on to the colonial legislative bodies, asking that they "be given the sanction of law at the earliest possible opportunity" (Temperley, 11). The measures included giving slaves more of an opportunity for religious instruction, removing obstacles to manumission (an issue we observe at work with Mary Prince), keeping slave families together, and regulating flogging more carefully and discontinuing the practice altogether for women. The abolitionists were none too satisfied with this arrangement:

The adoption of these somewhat vague proposals, which were
to constitute the basis of official policy for the next decade, did

little to placate the abolitionists. It was plain that in delegating responsibility to the colonies the Government was evading the issue. Nevertheless, it was now committed to taking some action. (Temperley, 11)

This caused a virtual standoff between the Parliament and the colonial legislatures regarding who had jurisdiction over, and best knew how to make decisions for, the colonies. The colonies, especially the Jamaican legislature, accused the British government of taking the side of the enemies of the colonies:

The lines were now clearly drawn. In the years that followed the pattern became only too familiar: Government instructions; opposition by the Assemblies; irresponsible acts of violence; strenuous denunciation on the part of the Anti-Slavery Society leading to more Government instructions and more opposition. (Temperley, 12)

Given this standoff between the colonies and the British government, it became apparent to some of the members of the Anti-Slavery Society that they could not hope to accomplish even their goal of gradual emancipation through appeal to Parliament alone. Some members wanted to appeal more directly to the people of England through a grassroots effort. In this way they would bring public opinion to bear on the Parliament for its actions. There was some resistance to this move in the group by more conservative members, such as Buxton, but even these members were convinced that such efforts were not antithetical to their own. Hence, in 1831 the Anti-Slavery Society established a subcommittee known as the Agency Committee. The committee hired a group of lecturers and sent them to speak in specific districts in order to rouse public sentiment and support for their cause. The committee's methods had "much in common with those used by religious revivalists. In adapting them to the needs of the anti-slavery cause, it [the committee] established a new highly effective technique later used with even greater effect in the United States" (Temperley, 13). The committee's efforts were so successful that, in the summer of 1832, it officially separated from the Anti-Slavery Society to become an independent organization. The society, though glad to see public sentiment being stirred up, was suspicious of the influence of the Agency Committee and still believed that working through Parliament was the best way to reach its goals. The Agency Committee was suspicious of the conservatism of the society, which it thought had erred in two ways:

> It had limited its emotional appeal to what they regarded as a select group of 'pious sentimentalists' . . . which was not only detached from the people but actually distrusted by them, and, at the same time, by thinking too much in terms of what Parliament would or would not accept, had confused the moral issue of slavery with questions of political and economic expediency. (Temperley, 14)

Perhaps no one commented so clearly on the workings and the politics of the Agency Committee as did George Stephen, in a letter to Harriet Beecher Stowe. In this letter, Stephen credits the committee with the foresight to understand the importance of public opinion in defeating slavery, but even more important, he lauds it for the technique of basing its ideology in religious duty:

> The value of popular feeling can be no mystery to you in the United States, but the ready descent from high aristocratic exclusiveness to the vulgar arts wherewith popular feeling is courted on the eve of an election, is not likely to be as well understood on your side of the water. . . .

> This was well understood by the Agency committee, and it was to secure the aid of this providential respectability that all their efforts were directed: their whole scheme of lecturing, of organizing affiliated societies, and of doing both on the principle of religious duty, was based upon this foundation. It was self-evident that if the religious world could be induced to enter upon the subject, severing it from all its political relations, and viewing it simply as a question between God and man, the battle was won; religious consistency is the essence of that which we call respectability of character.[27]

Stephen's words are informative here not only for what they suggest about the history of the Agency Committee but also for what they suggest about the status of abolitionist discourse. He recognizes "the subject" of slavery as a discursive site that can be positioned, taken up or argued in different ways. His assertion that if it were severed "from all political relations" and argued exclusively on the basis of not just religion but "religious duty," then "the battle was won" is especially revealing. To state this in terms that may have particular resonance for the modern-day reader, Stephen is arguing that the Agency Committee knew what today's religious right knows all too well. If the committee could convince a people trained, socialized, and conditioned for the rhetoric and ideology of religion that putting an end to slavery was their "religious duty," the "battle was won" indeed. The use of religious rhetoric in abolitionist discourse is itself a complicated issue, deserving of much longer treatment than provided here. In chapter 4, I address more specifically some of the religious and moral arguments that were waged around the issue of slavery, and I also briefly consider Douglass's position on religion in chapter 6.

In 1832, the anti-slavery campaign was aided by the concomitant struggle over parliamentary reform:

> The excitement over . . . the passage of the Reform Bill in June,
> the subsequent dissolution of Parliament, and the prepara-
> tions for a general election, led to a general feeling of exhila-
> ration. Reform was in the air and for the moment there was no
> clear idea of where it would end. (Temperley, 16)

Indeed, when the Parliament reassembled in January 1833, after the December 1832 election, abolitionists were delighted at the character of the new Parliament. It was evident that the abolitionists' efforts to support members who would be sympathetic to their cause had been successful. Through a series of political negotiations, on August 29, 1833, Parliament passed a bill, though not entirely satisfying to abolitionist leaders, that emancipated the slaves in British dominions. Part of the agreement was that provisions would be made to compensate the planters for the economic loss incurred by slave emancipation. This resulted in a policy of gradual emancipation, which included a period of apprenticeship of the slave to his or her master. The length of this period was highly contested. Some abolitionists, such as Stephen, were outraged that remunerations would be made at all to the planters for participation in a system that was now determined to be unlawful and immoral. Yet the effects of abolitionists' efforts can be seen in the development of the legislation. While Parliament's original proposal required eleven years of apprenticeship in the case of agricultural slaves and six years for domestic slaves, the final measure required only six years for agricultural slaves and four years for domestics.

After emancipation, not all abolitionists folded their tents and went home. Many continued, under the auspices of newly founded organizations, not only to ensure that the British government made good on its bill of emancipation but also to work toward universal abolition with their European neighbors and the United States. Efforts such as these, along with the campaigns already described, further attest to the need for a more cosmo-politan understanding of abolitionism and of abolitionist dis-course. What follows both here and after the companion overview of abolitionism's rise in the United States is a sampling of some of the principal and recurring themes raised by white abolitionists. These, in turn, provide some context for the con-sideration of slave testimony that follows this chapter.

### African Humanity and the Possibility of Rage in Edgeworth, Cowper, and Opie

It is well established, by scholars as wide-ranging as David Brion Davis in *The Problem of Slavery in Western Culture*, Moira Fer-guson in *Subject to Others*, and, more recently, Clare Midgley in *Women against Slavery*, that imaginative writings, especially poetry, by men and women in England had a great impact on the aboli-tionist movement. These were in no way, of course, the only means, nor even the primary means, by which abolitionists took their struggle to the threshold of the public door. Newspapers, political tracts, broadsides, public meetings, essays, sermons, and slave narratives were all methods that were used frequently and effectively. Midgley puts it best, perhaps, when she says that "as a complement to the tracts and pamphlets written almost exclu-sively by men, poetry by both sexes could, as D. B. Davis has pointed out, give 'a directness and emotional intensity to rational arguments that had long been ignored'. In this way 'masculine' reason and 'feminine' sensibility were enlisted as complemen-tary qualities in the fight against the slave trade."[28] Indeed, Midg-ley further suggests that during the Romantic period, with its in-creasing cultural emphasis on sentimentality, what we witness is the "feminisation of poetry and its democratisation . . . which was marked by the evolution of new styles which, in comparison to poetry of the Augustan Age, placed less stress on classical learning and set forms than on the expression of heartfelt sentiment and of natural talent" (32).

Midgley contends that tragic tales of romantic love between Africans, such as Eliza Knipe's narrative poem "Atombaka and Omaza: An African Story," in which an African warrior chief and his lover, while wrapped in each other's arms, throw themselves into the sea to drown rather than become slaves, would "foster sympathy for black suffering and awareness of black resistance and helped combat pro-slavery stereotypes of black men and women's animal sexuality and licentiousness" (33). Similarly, I argue here that the carefully executed and negotiated creation of imaginative black characters who could express rage attested to the humanity of the African. One of the challenges, then, that nineteenth-century abolitionist writers faced was how to represent the slave as sympathetic and reasonable without subsuming his or her humanity. Put another way, the slave's expression of rage, anger, and frustration toward what can only be described as the subhuman condition of slavery is an expression of his or her humanity. It would be, in fact, inhuman to respond in any other way to such extreme circumstances. The question of how to represent the African was made even trickier after 1791 and the revolt of Saint-Domingue, which rendered representations of black rage suspect and dangerous in the minds of a cautious public. I here briefly consider three literary examples, spanning chronologically the late eighteenth century to the early nineteenth century, that attempt such a negotiation: Maria Edgeworth's story "The Grateful Negro" (1802), William Cowper's poem "The Negro's Complaint" (1778), and Amelia Opie's poem "The Black Man's Lament, or, How to Make Sugar" (1826).

Let me begin with the text among these that I find to be simultaneously the most interesting and the most troubling, Edgeworth's "The Grateful Negro," which is one of the most densely allusive of the tracts I study here.[29] In fact, one can only marvel at how much Edgeworth manages to accomplish in the space of only eighteen pages, dense with allusions to Shakespeare and the Bible. She tells the story of two neighboring plantations in Jamaica—the Jeffries plantation and the Edwards plantation. Mr. Edwards is the classically "good" master and Mr. Jeffries the classically "bad" master in the tale. Needing to raise money, Jeffries orders the provision-grounds of Caesar (one of his most devoted and obedient slaves) and his wife, Clara, to be seized and the two of them to be sold. Edwards, learning of their fate and perceiving their grief, appeals to Jeffries and offers to buy both of them for the highest price offered at market. Jeffries agrees to the arrangement, and Caesar and Clara are taken to the Edwards plantation and given new provision-grounds and a house. Edwards assures Caesar with these words: "Now, my good friend . . . you may work for yourself, without fear that what you earn may be taken from you; or that you should ever be sold to pay your master's debts."[30] On hearing this proclamation, Caesar's "feelings were . . . so strong that he could not find expression for his gratitude; he stood like one stupefied! Kindness was new to him; it overpowered his manly heart; and at hearing the words 'my good friend,' the tears gushed from his eyes" (549). The major conflict in the story arises from the fact that the slaves on the Jeffries plantation, led by Hector (Caesar's devoted friend and countryman), have an elaborate plan for insurrection that designs to seize the entire island. Caesar, up to this moment, has been a co-conspirator with Hector, but now the feeling of "gratitude" overpowers all other emotions, and he wants to spare the life of his new master. So he entreats Hector to abandon their revolutionary plans. Hector refuses to do so and tries to use the magical influences of Esther, the Obeah woman, to change Caesar's mind.

Through various machinations, Caesar is forced into deciding whether to support the insurrectionists or to protect his master. He chooses the latter and warns his master of the attack, entreating him to arm himself and his slaves, who will protect him. On receiving a promise from his master that his friend Hector will be pardoned, Caesar leads Edwards and his band to Esther's house, where Hector and his compatriots are being prepared for battle by the Obeah woman. Edwards's contingent surrounds the house and burn the insurrectionists out. Hector, full of rage and the thirst for revenge, charges at Caesar and stabs him. Caesar survives. Mr. Edwards manages to quell the revolt and head it off before it goes beyond the Jeffries plantation. Jeffries and his family are forced, by the loss of more than £50,000, to return to England "to live in obscurity and indigence" (555). Edgeworth concludes the story by saying: "They had no consolation, in their misfortunes, but that of railing at the treachery of the whole race of slaves.—Our readers, we hope, will think that at least one exception may be made, in favor of THE GRATEFUL NEGRO" (555).

Describing Edgeworth's position with regard to her text, Anne K. Mellor in *Romanticism and Gender* explains that both Edgeworth and her father conceived of their Irish peasants and, by extension, their black West Indian slaves as "children, who needed to be well treated, with justice and benevolence and understanding, to be educated in honesty, Christian morality and especially obedience, but who could not yet be granted the freedoms and responsibilities of adulthood" (Mellor, 78). To demonstrate that Edgeworth equates the position of West Indian slaves with that of Irish tenant farmers, Mellor further explains:

> Explicit in this story is Edgeworth's conviction that the enlightened members of the ruling class, whether white slave owners or, by extension to Ireland, the Anglo-Irish Protestant Ascendancy, have the right as well as the obligation to control the lower classes. As [Michael] Hurst suggests, "she [Edgeworth] saw her role as something between a colonial civil servant and a missionary rescuing the masses from inferior

material and spiritual practices. Priestly witch-doctors [or the Obeah woman Esther] and the mumbo-jumbo of the old Irish language she regarded with the same scorn as [Thomas] Macaulay did the customs of the 'Hindoos.'" That Maria Edgeworth equated the position of West Indian slaves with those of nineteenth-century Irish tenant-farmers is clarified in her *Essay on Irish Bulls* where she quotes with approval Voltaire's comment in his *Age of Louis XIV* that:

Some nations seem made to be subject to others. The English have always had over the Irish the superiority of genius, wealth, and arms. The *superiority which the whites have over the negroes.* (Mellor, 79)

I think Mellor is right in her assessment of Edgeworth's racial intent or ideological investment in what Rudyard Kipling called the "white man's burden." This raises some pressing issues that bear further discussion. For instance, how does Edgeworth's equation of slaves with children connect with the discourse of amelioration that had currency at the time of the story's publication in 1802? Before considering this question, however, I examine how the figure of the Negro functions in Edgeworth's writing of white subjectivity. Let me bracket for a moment the fact that Edgeworth gives her moral approbation to Caesar (the grateful Negro) and concentrate more squarely on the politics between, and the relationship of, Caesar and Hector. If we take their respective positions seriously, what is the nature of the political struggle that divides them?

One way in which we might think about the differences between Hector and Caesar is that the first operates within a politics of institution while the latter operates within a politics of individuals. In the prior case, it is far easier to be decisive in terms of one's political action. Hector is unwavering in his purpose and design. He is clear about who constitutes the hegemonic block to be resisted—white people.[31] When we work within a politics of institution, we do not take account of individuals but rather of how they are "interpellated," that is, of their position in the cultural matrix, of their representational self. Since the institution of slavery is itself based, in part, on a complicated dialectic between slave (Negro) and master (white), certain benefits are derived in such an institution by virtue of one's whiteness. In purely institutional logic, it matters little whether one is a "good master" or a "bad master." What matters is that one *is* master.

It is readily apparent why the politics of individuals would earn Edgeworth's approbation. Steeped in an ideology that allows for the master to maintain authority and superiority (even as caretaker) while winning the gratitude of those who are in servitude to him or her, it constitutes a variation on the Hegelian master-slave dialectic, in which the Other is not annihilated but rather is taken into the self, consumed by the self. It is, after all, Mr. Edwards's subjectivity that is buttressed at the end of the story. He wins Caesar's devotion through his kindness. He wins the devotion of all his slaves, who protect him and help him to quell the insurrection. Caesar is part of the material for this masterful self-making and thereby wins the author's approbation at the close of the text. Caesar is useful precisely because he has acted out of gratitude to his master—a gesture that finally speaks well of Mr. Edwards and says little for Caesar. Or perhaps the gesture suggests that the only proper subjectivity for the slave is found in servitude.

Equally complicated in this narrative is the stabbing of Caesar by Hector. For the modern-day reader, this episode raises a number of contemporary concerns about black-on-black violence that I think are operable here. Many have speculated that the high rate of black-on-black crime in the United States is due to geography—that is, spaces that are ethnically and economically overdetermined. If crimes of passion (and here I mean crimes committed out of economic and social frustration and disenfranchisement) are going to be committed, they will be committed in those spaces to which, and against those people to whom, those committing them have access. (Consider the 1992 uprising in Los Angeles.) Caesar, having literally and metaphorically positioned himself between the insurrectionists and Mr. Edwards, becomes the available target of Hector's knife. Here, as we see all too often today, revenge, rage, and frustration are displaced or determined by access. This also demonstrates what being good to your slaves will get you. If you gain their gratitude, incorporate them into your self, they will protect you from all harm and danger.

But what of Caesar? What are his thoughts and motives? In the text, Edgeworth on three occasions describes the battle being waged in Caesar's mind over what action he should take. First, the narrator describes his disposition during his conversation with Hector:

> Caesar's mind was divided, between love for his friend and gratitude for his master: the conflict was violent and painful. Gratitude at last prevailed: he repeated his declaration, that he would rather die than continue in a conspiracy against his benefactor. (550)

The second description of Caesar's mental conflict is precipitated by Mr. Edwards giving him a knife in a show of trust:

> The principle of gratitude conquered every other sensation. The mind of Caesar was not insensible to the charms of freedom: he knew the Negro conspirators had so taken their measures that there was the greatest probability of their success. His heart beat high at the idea of recovering his liberty; but he was not to be seduced from his duty, not even by this delightful

hope; nor was he to be intimidated by the dreadful certainty
that his former friends and countrymen, considering him as a
deserter from their cause, would become his bitterest enemies.
The loss of Hector's esteem and affection was deeply felt by
Caesar. (553)

The final description occurs when Caesar is negotiating with Esther for the life of Clara, whom she has placed under her power,
just before he pretends to submit to Esther's will:

The conflict in his mind was violent; but his sense of gratitude
and duty could not be shaken by hope, fear, or ambition: nor
could it be vanquished by love. He determined, however, to appear to yield. (554)

Yet, when we get to the supposed joy that Caesar feels at the
end of the text, our narrator leaves it untold. We are informed
that "we must leave that to the imagination" (555). Are we to believe that Caesar (who has been represented as psychically em-
battled throughout the story) at the close of this text experiences
joy? How can this be? Are we also then to believe that he simply
forgets the problematic role he played in giving up his "countrymen" in the insurrection? This seems a curious conclusion at
best. Perhaps the narrator does not expand on Caesar's joy because it would be difficult, in the complicated terms in which
Caesar's character has been defined, to narrate his response to
all that has transpired by the story's end as one solely of joy.

The refusal to narrate Caesar's joy implicates the reader in the
underlying ideology of the story. The statement itself, "Caesar's
joy!—We must leave that to the imagination," is performative. It
fulfills the very thing it names—Caesar's joy. It compels the
reader toward the conclusion of the statement, despite any narrative evidence to the contrary. Indeed, if joy is not the reader's

anticipated character response for Caesar at the story's close, the narrator effectively cues the reader that it should be.

But what of the underlying ideology of the story? Edgeworth's characters are types functioning in a moral allegory. The moral sentiment in the story is not, strictly speaking, an abolitionist one. Instead, the story appears to argue for an ameliorationist stance toward slavery. It achieves this aim through the use of types and what those types, taken together, suggest about human morality. Hector is the vengeful, bad product of senses dulled by slavery. Caesar, in contrast, through the acts of kindness shown to him by his new master, literally experiences a change of heart and becomes a loyal slave. Mr. Jeffries is a gentleman blinded by the habituated dulling of the moral sense that is caused by slavery. Mr. Edwards is a humanitarian who wishes "that there was no such thing as slavery" and who shares the white man's burden. Edwards "was convinced, by the arguments of those who have the best means of obtaining information, that the sudden emancipation of the negroes would rather increase than diminish their misery." Therefore, he confined his "benevolence . . . within the bounds of reason" (547). His attitudes being what they are, the narrator tells us that Edwards "adopted those plans for the melioration of the state of the slaves, which appeared to him most likely to succeed, without producing any violent agitation of revolution" (547). Edwards is represented as the veritable paragon of amelioration, in a story where amelioration receives final moral approbation.

Edgeworth presents the human mind as a *tabula rasa*, the state of which is determined by human experience. It is the difference in experiences and moralizing influences that creates each of the types represented by Hector, Caesar, Jeffries, and Edwards. The chief example of this appears when Mr. Jeffries, in his inebriated and wanton state, does nothing to forbid the brutal beatings of the three men alongside Hector by the overseer Durant:

Yet so false are the general estimates of character, that all these gentlemen [the planters] passed for men of great feeling and generosity! The human mind, in certain situations, becomes so accustomed to ideas of tyranny and cruelty, that they no longer appear extraordinary or detestable; they rather seem part of the necessary and immutable order of things. (553)

Here morality is determined, at least in part, by the circumstances of life, which become normalized or come to appear as the "immutable order of things."

Earlier in the story, in the first narrative descriptions of Jeffries and Edwards, their moral positions are constructed on the basis of their experiences and their respective moral-philosophical socialization. To consider a few brief examples: The narrator's first words about Mr. Jeffries are that he "considered the negroes as an inferior species, incapable of gratitude, disposed to treachery, and to be roused from their natural indolence only by force" (546). The narrator's first descriptive words of Edwards are that "this gentleman treated his slaves with all possible humanity and kindness" (547). Jeffries represents the classic position of the planter class, whereas Edwards is the classic ameliorationist. The long conversation between Jeffries and Edwards, which turns quickly into a civil debate, is also telling. Consider this moment:

"Well, well!" retorted Jeffries, a little impatiently, "as yet, the law is on our side. I can do nothing in this business, nor you neither."

"Yes, we can do something; we can endeavor to make our negroes as happy as possible." (548)

Again, the different positions of the two men are fortified in this passage. I do not ignore the inherent contradiction in Jeffries's rhetorical appeal to "the law." To say that the law is "on our side" is not only to suggest a competition but also to point up the very malleability of the law. The nature of competition is that you take a risk because you can win today but lose tomorrow. This runs counter to the declaration "I can do nothing in this business," which suggests that slavery is a part of the systemic, natural order of things, or at least that it is beyond the means of any single individual to change. In fact, it seems as if Edgeworth creates an image of amelioration itself. Jeffries's prejudices are treated as a version of necessity that Edwards's reform cannot alter, or they at least provide a limit to reform. These kinds of circuitous logic, as I hope to show, are a staple feature of racialized discourse to which abolitionists were compelled to respond, and in terms of which they were required to articulate their positions.

I have already cited evidence to support Caesar's mental state, but it remains to say a word about Hector's:

> Revenge was the ruling passion of Hector: in Caesar's mind, it was rather a principle instilled by education. The one considered it as a duty, the other felt it as a pleasure. Hector's sense of injury was acute in the extreme; he knew not how to forgive. Caesar's sensibility was yet more alive to kindness than to insult. Hector would sacrifice his life to extirpate an enemy. Caesar would devote himself for the defense of a friend; and Caesar now considered a white man his friend. (550)

Hector's ruling passion is revenge. It directs his every thought and even consumes his dreams, as the text indicates (550). The difference for Caesar is that he learned the emotion of revenge ("instilled by education") from his slave experiences under Jeffries. Caesar is still able to be moved by individual acts of kindness to reconsider the case for the morality of whites; Hector cannot be moved. He thinks institutionally and in terms of received labels, but for Caesar, the nomenclature of slavery is not always appropriate for all individuals. Consider a conversation between the two, when Caesar entreats Hector to abandon his plans for revolution:

> "I could not sleep—without speaking to you on—a subject that weighs upon my mind. You have seen Mr. Edwards?"
>
> "Yes. He that is now your master."
>
> "He that is now my benefactor! My friend!"
>
> "Friend! Can you call a white man friend?" cried Hector, starting up with a look of astonishment and indignation.
>
> "Yes," replied Caesar, with firmness. "And you would speak, ay, and would feel as I do, Hector, if you knew this white man! Oh, how unlike he is to all of his race, that we have ever seen! Do not turn from me with so much disdain! Hear me with patience, my friend!" (550)

Significantly, the conversation here is about language, categories, and their moral and political import. Even the debate over how to name Mr. Edwards is suggestive. Caesar calls him "Mr. Edwards"; Hector refers to him as "your master"; Caesar responds by labeling him "My benefactor! My friend!" One attempts to humanize the individual, Mr. Edwards, while the other is determined to relegate him to the class with which dominant slave nomenclature and ideology associate him. It is in this context that Hector's question to Caesar, "Can you call a white man friend?" becomes all the more poignant. The question not only interrogates Caesar's morality and change of mind, but it also interrogates the possibility of a "white man" ever having access to the appellation or class of "friend" in relation to a slave. The rhetorical and political stakes here are high, since in the quoted passage Caesar calls both Edwards and Hector "friend." This is a classification that could only appear incorrect, as well as morally and politically repugnant, to Hector. It appears that Edgeworth's story, which finally disapproves of characters such as Jeffries and his overseer Durant, does not disapprove of slavery itself. In fact, in its moral approbation of Caesar and disapproval of Hector, the story, unlike the position to the contrary taken in Equiano's narrative (to be discussed in chapter 4), refuses to justify the anger or rage of Hector to the point of retaliation.

The common thread in the texts by Edgeworth, Cowper, and Opie is that each author is really far more invested in white subjectivity than in the plight of the Negroes each addresses. This is not a facile way to dismiss them or their place in abolitionist discourse. Rather, I read them in this way to point out that this representational dilemma is a persistent problem in abolitionist discourse. Nor do I mean that the character of these authors' respective representational politics with regard to the slave is the same. On the contrary, whereas Edgeworth represents black rage (in the figure of Hector) as an evil, Cowper's "The Negro's Complaint" subsumes rage within the superior virtue of reason. This Cowper achieves by having the Negro speak in the form of a complaint, or a rational moral argument, that takes the terms of pro-slavery rhetoric and turns them back on themselves. There is no threat of physical, retaliatory violence on the part of Cowper's Negro speaker. While Cowper's rational portrayal of the African as speaker and as tutored mind is an effort to humanize the African and to combat the Enlightenment claims of the apologist for slavery, this method also dehumanizes Africans by denying them a very understandable, human response—rage—to the kind of torture and subhuman conditions to which they are subjected. Consider this passage from Cowper's "The Negro's Complaint":

*Men from Europe bought and sold me,*
*Paid my price in paltry gold;*
*But, though slave they have enroll'd me,*
*Minds are never to be sold.*

*Still in thought as free as ever,*
*What are England's rights, I ask,*
*Me from my delights to sever*
*Me to torture, me to task?*

*Fleecy locks and black complexion*
*Cannot forfeit Nature's claim;*[32]
*Skins may differ, but affection*
*Dwells in white and black the same.* (lines 4–16)[33]

Designed primarily to call whites to their own higher morality by showing them what slavery does to a character as sympathetic as the poem's speaker, the complaint functions to address the effects of slavery on white subjectivity. Nevertheless, this complaint is still poignant in its way.

First, the sentimentality of the poem renders the speaker sympathetic. This is enhanced by the severe use of the economic metaphors of greed to characterize the Europeans who deal in slave trade: "Forc'd from home and all its pleasures, / Afric's coast I left forlorn; / To increase a stranger's treasures, / O'er the raging billows borne" (lines 1-4) The trajectory of this stanza, like the rest of the poem, is from innocence into the economic, marred by its associations with greed and torture. There is also an appeal in the poem to the "mind" as the reason for the African's humanity: "But, though slave they have enroll'd me / Minds are never to be sold. / Still in thought as free as ever, / What are England's rights, I ask, / Me from my delights to sever, / Me to torture, me to task?" (lines 7–12). The speaker asserts the seat of reason, the mind, as that which cannot be sold. If the mind cannot be commodified, then the speaker is also suggesting the possibility of an independent will on the part of the slave. These lines, taken with the stanza immediately following, further position slavery as a corporeal fact. It acts on, indeed is made possible by, corporeality, which includes complexion and other physical attributes (lines 13–14). The self, then, to which the speaker appeals when he says "Me" in lines 11 and 12 is a mental self, a self of the mind—because the mind (that is, the reason and accompanying human emotions and "affection[s]") "dwells in white and black the same." The Rousseauist appeal to the natural state of all humankind as being one of equality is important to the Negro's logic of inner equality, which reads all outward or "racial" difference as complete construction. In fact, the reason he can make this "complaint" at all is because he is "still in thought as free as ever" (11).

Finally, the two closing stanzas of the poem reinscribe the black-white racial dichotomy, which is all too familiar a strain in abolitionist discourse:

> *Deem our nations brutes no longer,*
> *Till some reason ye shall find*
> *Worthier of regard, and stronger*
> *Than the colour of our kind.*
>
> *Slaves of gold, whose sordid dealings*
> *Tarnish all your boasted pow'rs.*
> *Prove that you have human feelings,*
> *Ere you proudly question ours!* (lines 49–56)

These stanzas, like much of the rest of the poem, beg to be read ironically. By challenging his imagined audience of slaveholders or those sympathetic to slavery to find a better reason than skin color to justify calling Africans brutes, the Negro speaker—his intellect and humanity indicated by the sophistication of the "complaint" itself—points out the constructedness of "race." By turning the appellation "slave" back onto European readers, calling them "slaves of gold," he reiterates the economic greed that underlies slavery and makes those who participate in that institution the ones who have been robbed of their humanity: "Prove that you have human feelings, / Ere you proudly question ours!"

Like Cowper's poem, Opie's "The Black Man's Lament" is a strong example of sentimental moralizing. While its irony is much to be appreciated, it seems finally to be in the service of the same portrayal of the African as pitiable and threatening only to the morality of Europeans. In fact, Opie, in the end, erases the possibility of black rage altogether in her Negro speaker by exacting a high moral price for it.

While Opie follows Cowper in her valorization of the patience of the Negro, she does at least introduce the Negro's potential for rage, even if she finally closes it off as a moral option. In addition, she presents the specificity of slave oppression, arguing against those who would equate the lot of English peasants with that of the slave. On the issue of rage, let us consider this passage from the conclusion of "The Black Man's Lament, or, How to Make Sugar":

> *Well, I must learn to bear my pain;*
> *And lately I am grown more calm;*
> *For Christian men come o'er the main,*
> *To pour in Negro soul a balm.*
>
> *They tell us there is one above*
> *Who died to save both bond and free;*
> *And who, with eyes of equal love,*
> *Beholds White man and humble me.*
>
> *They tell me if, with patient heart,*
> *I bear my wrongs from day to day,*
> *I shall, at death, to realms depart,*
> *Where God wipes every tear away!*

*Yet still, at times, with fear I shrink;*
*For, when with sense of injury prest,*
*I burn with rage! and then I think*
*I ne'er can gain that place of rest.* (lines 153–172)[34]

While Opie allows for the possibility of the Negro's experience of rage, her theology also assesses a penalty for such passion: the possible loss of eschatological fulfillment or retribution (if that term is even appropriate here). The poem is aptly titled. As the Negro's "lament," it moralizes only implicitly. It never explicitly exacts a moral price from white slaveholders, as Cowper does, for their participation in slavery. Opie's lament, true to Quaker form, is all moral sentimentalizing. Moreover, the only moment when the ramifications for actions taken are made explicit is when the speaker refers to his rage. It is clear from the stanza preceding the reference that the speaker's regard for God is learned from "Christian men." These men have taught him a pacifist morality: "They tell me if, with patient heart, / I bear my wrongs from day to day, / I shall, at death, to realms depart, / Where God wipes every tear away!" This forces him to police his own rage. The implication is that Christian morality is the only thing that stands between the slave and his rage, which could—without the Christian moralizing influence—express itself violently, as it does in Edgeworth's Hector. At the very least, Opie's "lament" is an argument for the moral education of the slaves. At most, it makes the slave a sympathetic figure and, through her advocacy of moral education, puts the slave one step closer to full inclusion in the society of humankind.

Opie's firm characterization of the difference between the oppression of the working class in Britain and the oppression of the African goes far to specify the material impacts of these two different forms of oppression (lines 61–148). This comparison of the English working class to the African slaves (and, later, the former slaves) persisted throughout the period. Most notably, perhaps, it surfaced again in Thomas Carlyle's *An Occasional Discourse on the Nigger Question* (1849), in which Carlyle represented lazy, post-emancipation blacks living well in the colonies and even letting fruits rot on the vine while poor people starved in England. This rhetoric was used to approve measures to impose taxes on the imports from the colonies and was also later picked up by the pro-slavery advocacy in the United States to argue for the continuance of slavery. Opie's Negro speaker, however, reminds the reader of the important differences that attributes such as freedom, self-ownership, self-determination, and the right to marry and to work for one's own keep make in one's life. These are all things English peasants can do while slaves cannot.

### On Whiteness and Humanity: The Example of Blake's "The Little Black Boy"

As I stated in chapter 1, one of the main arguments of the pro-slavery advocates for the justification of slavery was that Africans were not of the same variety of humanity as Europeans and were therefore fit for slavery. This is why abolitionists were constantly responding to this claim in their writings by showing examples of the humanity of the African. Nonetheless, in this overdetermined political and philosophical debate, the equating of humanity with whiteness persists. To shed further light on the repeated examples in slave literature of comparing Africans to whites for the purpose of demonstrating that Blacks are, indeed, like whites, we need look no further than William Blake's "The Little Black Boy" from his *Songs of Innocence*. The poem wastes no time establishing the boundary between the naive innocence of the speaker and the fallen experience of the reader, based on a reading of the opening stanza:

*My mother bore me in the southern wild,*
*And I am black, but O! my soul is white;*
*White as an angel is the English child:*
*But I am black as if bereav'd of light.*

It is immediately apparent that "black" and "white" as signs signify far more than hue or skin color. They ask us to think within a politically constructed, racialized discourse in which "white" is identified with angels and good and "black" with the absence of light.[35] The speaker recognizes his undeniable Otherness even in his intense and innocent desire to be white ("but O! my soul is white").

In the next four stanzas, the speaker's mother rationalizes their racial oppression by stating it as God's preparing them to learn "to bear the beams of love" that emanate from God in the divine presence. This is not altogether unrelated to a kind of passive theology of oppression and suffering that at different times has found popular expression in Christianity and even in pro-slavery rhetoric. Such a model places compensatory emphases in the world to come.[36] What is dramatic and at the same time pitiable about the mother's paradigmatic rationalization is that suffering becomes a necessary component to final redemption:

*For when our souls have learn'd the heat to bear*
*The cloud shall vanish we shall hear his voice.*
*Saying: come out from the grove my love and care,*
*And round my golden tent like lambs rejoice.*

According to the mother, it is only after a season of suffering that the category of race is eradicated. Or is it? The speaker's interpretation of his mother's remarks are quite revealing in this respect:

*When I from black and he from white cloud free,*
*And round the tent of God like lambs we joy:*
*I'll shade him from the heat till he can bear,*
*To lean in joy upon our Father's knee.*
*And then I'll stand and stroke his silver hair,*
*And be like him and he will then love me.*

When the speaker and the little English boy are both in the presence of God, the speaker will shade the English boy from the heat of God until he can bear it. After which time, he will stand and stroke the English boy's hair "and be like him" and be loved by him.

Even after they are both free from their respective "cloud[s]," the little black boy sees it as his role to shade the little English boy, who has not had to undergo the kind of suffering and preparation the black boy has to be in the presence of God. What is more telling is that even in the presence of God, when the racial "clouds" are no more, the remnants of oppression, of absolute, undeniable Otherness, remain in the black boy's ultimate desire to "be like him" (the English boy) and to be loved by him. There is nothing here to say that the self is the Other or that they can ever be in a harmonious unity with one another. On the contrary, the language of oppression, of Otherness, subverts any attempt at even an eschatological synthesis in the presence of God.[37] The unity that closes this poem is the same kind of curious dialectical unity or "omnisubjectivity" of which Leo Damrosch speaks.[38] The problem with such an easy identification of the self with the Other is that the hope of the little black boy never can be actually to become the equal of the little English boy. Rather, he can only hope to be *like* him.[39]

Blake's rhetoric reminds us of the currency of the rhetorical trope of shedding epidermal layers. It returns us to a kind of phenomenal question of the body. The black body is the referent, the signifier, the site of contestation, precisely because of how it gets used in the racist practices of pro-slavery advocacy and rearticulated in abolitionist texts. I continue to pursue this interest in the black body and the articulation of whiteness in the following discussion of U.S. abolitionist texts.

## Reflections on Abolitionist Discourse in the United States

Every influence of literature, of poetry, and of art, in our time is becoming more and more in unison with the great master chord of Christianity, "good will to man."

The poet, the painter, and the artist now seek out and embellish the common and gentler humanities of life, and, under the allurements of fiction, breathe a humanizing and subduing influence, favorable to the development of the great principles of Christian brotherhood.

—Harriet Beecher Stowe, "Preface," *Uncle Tom's Cabin*

This they would sing as a chorus to words which to many would seem unmeaning jargon, but which, nevertheless, were full of meaning to themselves. I have sometimes thought that the mere hearing of those songs would do more to impress some minds with the horrible character of slavery, than the reading of whole volumes of philosophy on the subject could do.

. . . If any one wishes to be impressed with the soul-killing effects of slavery, let him go to Colonel Lloyd's plantation, and, on allowance day, place himself in the deep pine woods, and there let him, in silence, analyze the sounds that shall pass through the chambers of his soul; and if he is not thus impressed, it will only be because "there is no flesh in his obdurate heart."                                                 —Frederick Douglass

Arguably, the first historical landmark of nineteenth-century America to have a tremendous influence on racialized discourse was the 1808 Slave Trade Act, which brought about the cessation of the international slave trade in the United States. Winthrop Jordan, in *White over Black*, suggests:

> Since opposition to slavery was widespread and in some quarters intense, tracing its decline and virtual collapse after official abolition of the slave trade in 1808 affords one basic periodization of fundamental changes in American thought after the Revolution. (xi)

And a change in thought it was. Lorenzo D. Turner tells us that prior to the passage of the 1808 Slave Trade Act, American literary opposition to slavery was based on passionate moral and religious arguments, which first appeared in the writings of Puritans and Quakers.[40] The period 1808 to 1830 was quite different, however. While the anti-slavery arguments of this period (which were much less frequent) are similar to those prior to 1808, they are far milder in their tone and in their passion. Turner points to Ralph Waldo Emerson as an example of this mildness (33).

Part of the reason for such a sharp decline in anti-slavery literature and the broader "cooling" of the anti-slavery movement is that anti-slavery proponents saw the cessation of the international slave trade as a huge victory, and many were content to simply rest on their laurels:

> During the years immediately following the passage of the Slave-Trade Act in 1808 arguments against slavery . . . were less frequent and on the whole milder in tone than those of the preceding period. The African slave-trade, to the abolition of which many writers of the first period had solely directed their

> efforts, had, in theory, at least, been abandoned. This period
> from 1808 to 1831 has been termed the period of preparation
> for Garrisonian abolitionism . . . which was to begin in 1831
> with William Lloyd Garrison [and his *Liberator*] as Leader.
> (Turner, 33)

Turner takes this claim about the 1808–31 period further by suggesting that most of the anti-slavery proponents who showed
interest in the slaves' welfare were concerned foremost with the
moral and religious instruction of the slaves. "Consequently,"
he says, "seeing slavery in opposition to this instruction, they
opposed slavery. Few . . . appear to have foreseen any serious
consequences that might result from the continuance of such a
system, and none of them effected any permanent plan for abolishing it" (3).

In 1831, William Lloyd Garrison began publishing *The Liberator*, his famous abolitionist newspaper. It should be noted that the
term *abolitionist* here is used with purpose, since Garrisonian abolitionism is of a completely different variety from the kind of anti-
slavery sentiment in the 1808–30 period. Garrison denounced
the very institution of slavery, calling for "complete and immediate freedom" for slaves; he demanded that the North repudiate
all association with the South and condemned the U.S. Constitution, calling it "a covenant with death and an agreement with
hell."[41] It was this variety of militant abolitionism, often referred
to as Garrisonian abolitionism, that took off under Garrison's
leadership between 1831 and 1865.

The period from 1850 to 1861 was the "second period of mil-
itant-abolitionism," evidenced by the fact that opposition to slavery in American literature during this eleven-year period was
greater and more effective than ever before in the anti-slavery
movement (Turner, 70). The reason for the radical increase in
the production of anti-slavery literature in this period was the

passage of the Fugitive Slave Act on September 18, 1850, and the subsequent attempts to enforce it, which revealed slavery in one of its worst forms. For a cogent example of the kind of horror caused by the Fugitive Slave Act, one need look no further than Margaret Garner, whose story was the basis for Toni Morrison's *Beloved*.[42] Turner cites Harriet Beecher Stowe's *Uncle Tom's Cabin* as "the first really significant reaction to this law." The anti-slavery arguments used in this period were still very much in the religious, moral, and sentimental vein, but "strong pleas for the abolition of slavery as a social, economic, and political necessity were not wanting" (70–71).

While the welfare of the slave remained a constant concern for the authors of anti-slavery literature in the Civil War period (1861–65), the issue of slavery took second place to a larger concern: the very life of the nation, "so dangerously near extinction." The opposition to slavery on moral, religious, social, and economic grounds was found most readily in the novel, while sentimental arguments were relegated almost completely to poetry (Turner, 106). Many of these publications were intended to boost the morale of those fighting the war for freedom and national unity. In 1863–64, for example, William Robinson writes in *Critical Essays on Phillis Wheatley*, the *Proceedings of the Massachusetts Historical Society* committed "many of its pages to the continuous printing of Wheatlyana." During these particular years, the society added to its credits the publishing of

a newly found Wheatley manuscript poem; a facsimile of her handwriting; two letters from manuscripts; an account of American reprintings of the 1773 volume through 1863; and documentation of Phillis's husband practicing law in Boston courtrooms. . . . In 1864 a member of that Society, Charles Deane, reprinted the seven Wheatley letters separately at his own expense. (*Critical Essays*, 9)

This was done in response to the Enlightenment claims that creative genius (evidenced through writing) was the litmus test for humanity.

The Reconstruction years, roughly 1865–76, were fraught with complications and contradictions—white, Northern liberalism; a frustrated, largely disenfranchised, white, Southern conservatism; legal, educational, political, and economic advancements for Blacks through the federal government and the Freedmen's Bureau; and the rise of Southern, white-supremacist groups to curtail "Negro and northern control," to name a few. The job of Reconstruction in the South, even in its most radical moments, was never stable. Many Southerners continued their resistance to Reconstruction because the rapid advancements that it called for on behalf of the Blacks were too much, too fast. John Hope Franklin states that after much conflict between the North and the South, which finally culminated in the election of Rutherford B. Hayes as president of the United States in 1876, the federal government ("in the spirit of conciliation") withdrew its troops and left the South to its own devices.[43]

According to August Meier, "The generation following the collapse of the Reconstruction governments and the Compromise of 1877 underwent a period of increasing discrimination, especially in the South."[44] Indeed, when the federal government acquiesced to white hegemony in the South, it left the Blacks with no one to protect their civil and political interests. Many events were precipitated by this course of action. Mississippi and South Carolina, in 1890 and 1895 respectively, became the first states to constitutionally disenfranchise Blacks after Reconstruction.[45] Lynchings, mostly in the South, reached a peak in the 1880s and early 1890s. Throughout the South, the universal segregation of schools (1870s and 1880s), public transportation (1880s and 1890s), and public facilities was realized. Since public opinion in the North had never been completely sympathetic to Blacks and the majority of Northerners had no delusions of racial equality, the scene was no brighter there. For example, only four Northern states admitted Blacks equally with whites to public schools in 1865 (Meier, 19–21).

It was not until 1880 that Blacks in the North completely won the right to an education, and not until 1900 that they achieved the integration of public schools (on paper). The years 1887–91 brought the first significant surge of Jim Crow laws with the rise to power in the legislatures of the Farmers' Alliance. By the 1890s a new imperialism was serving as a reinforcer of American racism. This culminated in the famous *Plessy v. Ferguson* decision, which maintained the doctrine of separate but equal. Meier contends that "Oriental exclusion, the Southern race system, the New Imperialism and racist Social Darwinism all combined to give the close of the nineteenth century and the opening of the twentieth an interesting configuration in regard to race relations" (20–23).

### Emerson and the Fugitive Slave Law: Toward a Theory of Whiteness

Dunbar, the young *erudit*, the Scottish scientist and man of letters, was no sadist. His plantation regime was, by the standards of the time, mild; he clothed and fed his slaves decently, and frequently relented in his more severe punishments. But 4,000 miles away from the sources of culture, alone on the far periphery of British civilization where physical survival was a daily struggle, where ruthless exploitation was a way of life, and where disorder, violence, and human degradation were commonplace, he had triumphed by successful adaptation. Endlessly enterprising and resourceful, his finer sensibilities dulled by the abrasions of frontier life, and feeling within himself a sense of authority and autonomy he had not known before, a force that flowed from his absolute control over the lives of others, he emerged a distinctive new man, a borderland gentleman, a man of property in a raw, half-savage world.

—Bernard Bailyn, *Voyagers to the West*

In *The Problem of Slavery in Western Culture,* David Brion Davis maintains that nineteenth-century writers on both sides of the Atlantic held an optimistic or progressive view of history with regard to slavery. "These writers," according to Davis, "saw modern slavery as a moral contradiction, a force incompatible with natural law, Christianity, the progress of scientific enlightenment, or the mission of American democracy."[46] Davis ultimately concludes, however, that these nineteenth-century writers tended to overemphasize the opposition between slavery and Christianity, since their position did not take account of the economic role slavery played in the United States' development.

In a brief comment on Ralph Waldo Emerson's "An Address in the Court-House in Concord, Massachusetts, on 1st August, 1844, on the Anniversary of the Emancipation of the British West Indies," Davis uses Emerson to demonstrate how nineteenth-century writers participated in this construction of an optimistic view of history. He quotes Emerson, who notes that "other revolutions have been the insurrection of the oppressed; this was the repentance of the tyrant." Hence, Davis asserts, according to Emerson, "British emancipation was both proof of moral progress in history and the harbinger of a new era" (26). Davis concludes his reading with a quote from Emerson on the Deity's role in the production of a progressive view of history: "The Power that built this fabric of things, has made a sign to the ages, of his will" (26).

I agree with Davis that recognition of the moral dilemma posed by slavery in the United States does not necessitate our acceptance that emancipation was "preordained by the pro-

gressive unfolding of moral truth, or that men of the nineteenth-century were morally superior to those in periods when
slavery was universally accepted, or that in the contest between
slaveholders and abolitionists all virtue and reasonableness
were on one side" (27). Furthermore, Davis's comments provide a useful background for the discussion to follow (if all too
truncated by the present summation). I do, however, take exception not so much to Davis's larger cultural argument as to
the rhetorical use to which he puts Emerson. My project here,
in part, is an attempt to extricate Emerson from the types of
overgeneralized claims made about him by Davis and others,
by distinguishing Emerson's position on slavery from that of
most nineteenth-century writers. While Emerson certainly participated in a morally informed and progressive view of history,
he did take account of the economic forces that drive slavery.
In addition, I argue that in his "Address on the Fugitive Slave
Law"[47] (written over a decade after the British West Indies
Emancipation anniversary address), Emerson accomplishes a
successful rhetorical negotiation of the politics of slavery and
educated white male subjectivity.

Rhetorically, a number of things in "The Address" fascinate
the reader and demonstrate the author's intellectual prowess. I
concentrate on the language Emerson uses to argue against the
passage of the Fugitive Slave Law. It should be immediately apparent to the careful reader that only to a very limited extent
does Emerson argue the plight of the slave in sentimental terms
in this text—an approach that certainly had much currency in
abolitionist discourse of the period. Instead, he grounds his rhetoric in a painstakingly honest and eloquent discourse about what
is positive and negative in white culture. That is, the slave is not
the material for Emerson's critique of the Fugitive Slave Law;
rather, Emerson grounds his critique in the effects of slavery
on white men and their cultural values. The remainder of this

discussion of Emerson, then, addresses the two principal passages in "The Address" in which we may read Emerson's construction of whiteness:

It [passage of the Fugitive Slave Law] showed that our prosperity had hurt us, and that we could not be shocked by crime.
It showed that the old religion and sense of the right had faded
and gone out; that while we reckoned ourselves a highly cultivated nation, our bellies had run away with our brains and the
principles of culture and progress did not exist.[48]

I have respect for conservatism. I know how deeply founded it
is in our nature, and how idle are all attempts to shake ourselves free from it. We are all conservatives, half Whig, half Democrat, in our essences; *and might as well try to jump out of our
skins as to escape from our Whigery.* There are two forces in Nature, by whose antagonism we exist; the power of Fate, Fortune, the laws of the world, the order of things, or however else
we choose to phrase it, the material necessities, on the one
hand,—and Will or Duty or Freedom on the other. (549; my
emphasis)

Emerson makes his intended audience clear on the first page of
his address: "My own habitual view is to the well-being of students
or scholars. And it is only when the public event affects them,
that it very seriously touches me. And what I have to say is to
them. For every man speaks mainly to a class whom he works with
and more or less represents. It is to these I am beforehand related and engaged, in this audience or out of it—to them and not
to others" (541). The relevance of this quote will, I trust, become
apparent as we proceed.

In the first quotation above, Emerson discusses what the passage of the Fugitive Slave Law reveals about the nature of white

men who have come to accept the reality of slavery. I consider, first, the use of the first-person plural pronoun and, second, the use of the clearly economic language. The use of the first-person plural pronoun is not ambiguous here. Considering the quote by Emerson about his imagined audience, I feel confident in reading a degree of specificity into the imagined community he evokes. "We" here designates a community of educated white men. This move to lay claim to a community of educated white men is at once politically progressive and disturbing. It is progressive when we consider that the context in which this community is being evoked and taken to task is in response to the passage of the Fugitive Slave Law. Instead of making an all-too-easy and routine appeal to the plight of the "poor African" (again, a gesture that was solidly a part of contemporary abolitionist vernacular), Emerson puts white men (himself included, I think) under the microscope in order that their role in this travesty may be examined.

It is disturbing because it is also very common in contemporary pro-slavery discourse to speak of white men as a community with capacities superior to Africans. While Emerson is doing something quite different in evoking this community of white men, I do not want to lose sight of the complex of real and rhetorical power relations implied by the evocation of a community of white men. It is troubling also because one cannot help thinking that Emerson's pronoun usage is similar to the way in which the first-person plural functions for marginalized or disempowered groups. Perhaps comments made by Barbara Johnson in a similar context can be instructive here:

> The pronoun "we" has historically proven to be the most empowering and shiftiest shifter of them all. It is through the "we" that discourses of false universality are created. With its cognitive indeterminacy and its performative authority, it is

both problematic and unavoidable for discourses of political opposition. For this structure of the stressed subject with an indeterminate predicate may well be the structure necessary for empowerment without essentialism. At the same time, it is an empowerment always in danger of presuming too much. But, then, can there be empowerment without presumption?[49]

Johnson's comments appear in the context of a response to Henry Louis Gates, Jr.'s use of this language of community to speak the terms of ownership of African American literature. While I am inclined to agree with Johnson that the pronoun *we* creates discourses of false universality and that it is "both problematic and unavoidable for discourses of political opposition," one must ask how this reading of "the shifter" changes when the speaker is not activating discourse from the margin but is speaking from the center. Must one—indeed, can one—distinguish between Emerson's oppositional position in responding to the Fugitive Slave Law and the conservative potential of the communal rhetoric of white maleness? Or perhaps the question is even more complicated: Can the question of Emerson's conservative communal rhetoric be divided into the conservatism of the rhetoric and the progressive use to which it is being put in providing a critique of white male subjectivity?

The other observation that should be made about the passage from Emerson is how he links the metaphors of economic greed to this community of white men:

[Passage of the Fugitive Slave Law] showed that our *prosperity* had hurt us, and we could not be shocked by crime. . . . That while we reckoned ourselves a highly cultivated nation, our *bellies* had run away with our brains and the principles of culture and progress did not exist. (548; my italics)

This critique of greed and prosperity is at least one important way in which Emerson distinguishes himself from Davis's earlier generalization about nineteenth-century writers' unwillingness to confront the economic role of slavery in the United States' development. And of course, Emerson's willingness to speak so candidly about greed as a part of white male subjectivity in the mid-nineteenth-century United States (*"our* prosperity," *"our* bellies") is a bold move toward defining cultural whiteness.

In the second passage to be considered, I call attention to the first three sentences:

> I have respect for conservatism. I know how deeply founded it is in *our* nature, and how idle are all attempts to shake *ourselves* free from it. *We* are all conservatives, half Whig, half Democrat, in *our essences; and might as well try to jump out of our skins as to escape from our Whigery.* (549; my italics)

Emerson's identification of conservatism as a tenet of white male identity is also a very bold move. When Emerson says that "he knows how deeply founded conservatism is in our nature," I do not read this as suggesting a biological essence to conservatism in white men. On the contrary, it is "in their nature" precisely because of their social position. Emerson's understanding of conservatism as overdetermined by social location is implied by his critiques of the Fugitive Slave Law and of slavery, which pervade this text. That is, white male conservatism is in part derived from the superiority white men feel toward Africans who are in slavery.

The final piece of evidence that argues for the white racial association Emerson is making to conservatism is in the last sentence quoted: "and might as well try to jump out of our skins as to escape from our Whigery." Some might read this as a fortunate or unfortunate cohering of metaphors. I, however, do not think it accidental. The obvious identification of the sign of racial marking—skin—with "Whigery" or "conservatism" is the most radical gesture Emerson makes with regard to his construction of whiteness in the text.[50] It bears reiteration here that all this happens in the context of a text that is a scathing response to the passage of the Fugitive Slave Law. What is most remarkable is that, instead of parading the image of the pitiful and pitiable slave onto the rhetorical stage in order to defend against the Fugitive Slave Law, Emerson chooses to address how "whiteness" (derived from the ideology of racial superiority) has given rise to the creation of the law and is advanced by it at the same time. Emerson's originality and radicality in his decision to choose this rhetorical strategy, against all established precedents to the contrary, more than warrants our attention. It shows a tremendous sensitivity and foresight to the future work that would need to be done in order to deconstruct the idea that slavery and racism are problems only for and about the African. Emerson points out the issues that are at stake for *white men* under the institution of slavery and slavery's impact on white cultural values.

Emerson, I am convinced, understands all too well the negative effects slavery has on the "cultivated sensibilities" of white men. Like the young Scottish scientist Dunbar, the man of letters in my epigraph to this section, the men Emerson describes are products of their social location in the system of slavery. This location, as Emerson effectively demonstrates, is precisely the thing that creates the reckless sense of "authority and autonomy . . . that flow[s] from . . . absolute control over the lives of others."[51] In at least one important sense, this address, for Emerson, is about how slavery is bad not only for what it does to the slave but also for what it does to the "cultivated master."[52] Emerson's discussion of the corruption of Daniel Webster, which occupies a great deal of the beginning of the address, was intended to make precisely this point—that no one is beyond danger of corruption by this peculiar social institution.

## Troping the Slave: Margaret Fuller's Review of Douglass's Narrative

Perhaps the most charitable and historicized reading of Margaret Fuller's review of the *Narrative of the Life of Frederick Douglass* would find Fuller's review to be a very radical statement for abolitionism. For the moment, however, I want to move from the level of meaning (i.e., what Fuller intends to say) to the level of ideology (i.e., how Fuller's rhetoric subverts her "meaning" and points out the ideological limitations by which she, even in her most radical of moments, is circumscribed). While Fuller intends her discussion of Douglass as a radical abolitionist statement, on careful examination we witness the ways in which ideology erupts, leaving her language to bear the trace of that eruption. Put another way, I want to show in the reading of Fuller how the radicality of her own abolitionist vision is limited by the very terms of the racialized discourse in which she must articulate herself.

It is important to understand the philosophical debate into which Fuller entered upon writing this review—a debate of which she and most abolitionists had full awareness. Henry Louis Gates, Jr., has argued in *Figures in Black*, in his introduction to *"Race," Writing and Difference*, and elsewhere that the Enlightenment brought about the union of reason with humanity. Concomitantly, Enlightenment thinkers used this idea to prove the inhumanity of the slave.[53] The argument in its most redacted form goes something like this: because reason is what defines humanity, and reason is manifested through literacy and the ability to write creatively, the African cannot be human, since he or she is incapable of creating imaginative texts. This reasoning goes far in explaining why Fuller's review spends so little time addressing the substance of Douglass's *Narrative*. Instead, Fuller rhetorically appropriates Douglass for her larger project: addressing the philosophical construction of African inhumanity. "Douglass" is writ large as an allegory for the ability and sensibility of the African, or more pointedly, "Douglass" is the material for the abolitionist discourse that truly interests Fuller:

> It is an excellent piece of writing and on that score to be prized as a specimen of the powers of the black race, which prejudice persists in disputing. We prize highly all evidence of this kind, and it is becoming more abundant. (Fuller, 379)

And indeed, the abolitionists did prize such "evidence" highly. Fuller is hardly unusual in how she makes use of Douglass's text and of "Douglass" as trope. Countless examples of this practice exist in the philosophical struggle to dismantle the institution of slavery. In fact, one could interrogate the extent to which African American literary production is linked to the white abolitionist desire for such texts.

Another moment of great interest in Fuller's review that speaks directly to this issue of the overdeterminacy of her ideological limitations comes after she introduces the excerpt from Douglass that concludes her review:

> We wish that every one may read his book, and see what a mind might have been stifled in bondage—what a man may be subjected to the insults of spendthrift dandies, or the blows of mercenary brutes, in whom there is no whiteness except of the skin, no humanity except in the outward form, and of whom the Avenger will not fail yet to demand, "Where is thy brother?" (381)

This passage is replete with interpretive possibilities. For the moment, however, I take up briefly the rhetorical status of "whiteness" and "humanity" in this passage, in an effort to demonstrate more clearly what I mean by Fuller's ideological limitations.

In this passage, Fuller implicitly lionizes whiteness as a kind of virtue. Placed in opposition to "spendthrift dandies" and "mercenary brutes," whiteness is posited as civility. Whiteness, in fact, is articulated as the measure of human civility. Fuller's discussion of whiteness is not a question of phenotype. This possibility is dismissed out of hand: "in whom there is no whiteness, except of the skin." In this rhetorical gesture, the sign "whiteness" as phenotype is completely emptied of meaning. It signifies nothing. Rather, Fuller's use of whiteness requires that we understand its socially constructed meaning, its ideological value. Whiteness is a stand-in here for all that is good about humankind. The problem becomes her inability to imagine an unracialized realm. In the context of a review that tries to mitigate racial difference, Fuller can only articulate the good as "whiteness." This rhetorical/imaginative impoverishment represents at least one of the ideological limitations of Fuller's radical project. Jenny Sharpe, in her excellent essay contribution to Mary Prince scholarship, "'Something Akin to Freedom': The Case of Mary Prince," puts the matter this way: "The antislavery position, like its pro-slavery counterpart, articulated a racial hierarchy, but one that was culturally rather than biologically determined" (33).

It remains to say a word about Fuller's rhetorical use of "humanity." She clearly disentangles "humanity" from the "outward form." Once again, we are not dealing with corporeality. So what, then, is Fuller calling on when she writes "humanity"? For this we need to consider what Fuller speculates would have been lost had Douglass remained in slavery: "We wish that every one may read his book, and see what kind of mind might have been stifled in bondage." "Humanity" for Fuller means the mind, mental energy. This desire for transcendence over the corporeal should remind us of Emerson's *Nature*—the metaphor of the transparent eyeball, the distinction between the Me and the Not Me. To put it in terms that Jesse Jackson might use: the measure of our humanity is not our corporeality but our mentality. Perhaps this is

Fuller's way of suggesting that it is the collusion of corporeality and racialization that ultimately enslaves the African. After all, slavery is possible only when there are material bodies to be enslaved. And though the Emersonian desire for transcendence is compelling in many contexts, it is, in the final analysis, perhaps impossible for us to imagine slavery among transparent eyeballs.[54] This reading is not intended by any means as a negative evaluation of Fuller. It is, rather, an opportunity for us to observe one of the rhetorical impoverishments of abolitionist discourse at work.

### The Body as Evidence: Garrison's Defense of David Walker's Appeal

In 1829, David Walker wrote and published his *Appeal to the Colored Citizens of the World, but in Particular and Very Expressly, to Those of the United States of America.* In the year after its publication, Walker died of causes unknown. There is still speculation about the circumstances surrounding his death. A bounty had been placed on his head by a group of men in the state of Georgia. Many laws were passed in the South banning "the circulation of seditious publications" and reiterating the policy against teaching slaves to write or read.[55] Such intense response to the *Appeal* attests to its centrality in the slavery debates. The text also warrants attention for how it redoubled white Southerners' fear of black literacy. Many Northern liberals were also scandalized by the angry tone of the *Appeal.* Even William Lloyd Garrison, as Truman Nelson tells us, was reluctant to take up the subject. But in 1831, shortly after publication of *The Liberator* had begun, Garrison was constantly under pressure to give his opinion on the pamphlet that was causing so much upheaval:

With the very first issue of the paper, Garrison was plunged into a dilemma which was to plague him all of his life: what to do about the black people who wanted to defend themselves against their oppressors. He had been in Boston when David Walker wrote his pamphlet calling on the slaves to rise up against their masters. Walker was greatly admired there among the people of color who were being profoundly affected by the tides of revolutionary liberation sweeping in from Europe. Garrison was constantly pressured to give his judgment on the Walker pamphlet. His judgment was rather ambiguous; he deplored the physical militancy of its spirit but felt it was a remarkable document in itself and completely justifiable in terms of the language whites used to each other at Fourth of July celebrations. It is interesting to contrast here the responses of Garrison and [Benjamin] Lundy to Walker. Lundy takes the customary pacifist position against any suggestions or appeals for violence, whether coming from the oppressed or the oppressor. This may be why Lundy never achieved a considerable following among the free blacks while Garrison's following was crucial and sustaining.[56]

I have already discussed briefly the role that *The Liberator* and its editor, William Lloyd Garrison, played in the radicalizing of American abolitionism. Now, in a very specific example from *The Liberator*, I take up Garrison's defense of David Walker's appeal. It is worth noting that Garrison's defense of Walker takes place in the context of the defense of white abolitionists against the common claims of the pro-slavery advocacy that the general resistance and unrest among slaves were caused by abolitionist agitation. Walker's body in particular, and the slave body in general, get posited between the warring white "countrymen." When Garrison states, "It is not *we* but our guilty countrymen, who put arguments into the mouths, and swords into the hands of slaves," he makes explicit the fact that his discourse is intended as a retort to the pro-slavery advocacy's blaming of the abolitionist for the riotous and militant behavior of slaves. In this way, Walker and his *Appeal* become the occasions for, or the discursive sites of, the abolitionist debate with the pro-slavery advocacy. Garrison's defense is also noteworthy for how it, like Fuller's review of Douglass, makes rhetorical use of Walker's black body. Garrison's rhetorical move is even more compelling if we place it alongside the rhetorical move of Benjamin Lundy,[57] another noted and committed American abolitionist figure and a contemporary of Garrison, who uses Walker's black body to take a more traditional, pacifist stance against the *Appeal*. Consider first the following passage by Garrison:

> If any people were ever justified in throwing off the yoke of their tyrants, the slaves are that people. It is not we [the abolitionists], but our guilty countrymen, who put arguments into the mouths, and swords into the hands of the slaves. Every sentence that they write—every word that they speak—every resistance that they make, against foreign oppression, is a call upon their slaves to destroy them. Every Fourth of July celebration must embitter and inflame the minds of the slaves. And the late dinners, and illuminations, and orations, and shoutings, at the south over the downfall of the French tyrant, Charles the Tenth, furnish so many reasons to the slaves why they should obtain their own rights by violence.
>
> Some editors have affected to doubt whether the deceased Walker wrote this pamphlet.—On this point skepticism need not stumble: the Appeal bears the strongest internal evidence of having emanated from his own mind. No white man could have written in language so natural and enthusiastic. (6)

This example is noteworthy, first, for how Garrison uses the rhetorical posture of speculation, or a conditional voice: "if any people were ever justified . . . ," "every Fourth of July celebration must embitter. . . ." At the same time that he presumes to speak for the slave, he recognizes the insufficiency and inauthenticity of his own voice in such matters. This recognition is demonstrated most clearly in the closing statement of the quote, when Garrison responds to the doubt or suspicion under which some editors have placed the authenticity of Walker's *Appeal:* "the Appeal bears the strongest internal evidence of having emanated from his own mind. No white man could have written in language so natural and enthusiastic." This statement recognizes the power of language to move and affect the politics of others. More importantly, Garrison recognizes that language does not exist solely at the level of abstract discourse or utterance, but that these utterances are also embodied. Still more radically, the statement recognizes—to return to a point of argument in chapter 1—that language emanates from bodies that bear meaning in the world. That is, Garrison suggests here that, at least in part, to interpret Walker's *Appeal* and to verify its authenticity is to account for, and quite literally to return to, the site of Walker's essentialized black body.[58] This appeal to the body becomes the evidence for the authenticity of Walker's *Appeal* itself.

Lundy, in contrast, takes a far more conservative position on the matter. In fact, in 1966, Truman Nelson, editor of *Documents of Upheaval,* justified the inclusion of Lundy's statement on the matter by saying that his "comments . . . [are] so typical of the liberal position on Negro 'violence' or 'self-defense' today, I cannot resist printing it here" (4). Nelson's words are as applicable today as they were in 1966, when he wrote them. Lundy's rhetorical strategy is to distance abolitionism from Walker's *Appeal.* He carves out a place for the "wise and good," who constitute the "our" of "our cause," who cannot possibly hold anything morally in common with the likes of Walker:

I had not seen this far-famed production until within a few days. A more bold, daring inflammatory publication, perhaps, never issued from the press, in any country. I can do no less than set the broadest seal of condemnation upon it. Such things can have no other earthly effect than to injure our cause. The writer indulges himself in the wildest strain of reckless fanaticism. He makes a great parade of technical phraseology, purporting to be religious; but religion has nothing at all to do with it. It is a labored attempt to rouse the worst passions of human nature, and inflames the minds of those to whom it is addressed. (In Nelson, 4)

First, Lundy justifies the reason for dignifying this subject. It has been "far-famed" and is, perhaps, according to Lundy, the worst production of its kind ever to appear in print. He maintains that "such things can have no earthly effect than to injure our cause." The "our" here is complicated in the way it shifts in Lundy's rhetoric. In this first sense, he intends "our" to mean "abolitionists'." They, after all, were the ones who had come under severe attack for rousing such revolutionary ideas among blacks.[59] "Our" here also dismisses the possibility that Walker has any connection to abolitionism. In fact, Lundy, like so many other white abolitionists, becomes the arbiter not only for what abolitionism is but of who has access to the category. Clearly, Blacks with revolutionary politics are unacceptable.

Lundy further contends that Walker "indulges himself in the wildest strain of reckless fanaticism" and that he "makes a great parade of technical phraseology, purporting to be religious." He concludes, however, that "religion has nothing at all to do with it," and that Walker is simply attempting to "rouse the worst passions of human nature and, inflame the minds of those to whom it is addressed." The same, with very little need for alteration, could be and indeed was said about the abolitionists by their opponents. George Stephen's comment to Harriet Beecher Stowe, which I referred to earlier, recognized the rhetorical strategy employed by the Agency Committee to make the public feel that ending slavery was part of their "religious duty." In this way, Walker's religious rhetoric and his revolutionary rhetoric both have strong precedents among his white American predecessors and contemporaries. One facet of Garrison's defense of Walker is that Walker follows in a very strong tradition that is not limited to abolitionists. What Lundy does, however, is represent Walker's position as aberrant—outside the abolitionist, religious, or moral purview—and therefore indefensible.

The last rhetorical move Lundy makes is, perhaps, classically liberal. He instructs "the colored race" on the best way to "obtain redress for their wrongs." He accomplishes this first, and most significantly, by seemingly identifying with Walker, saying that "the colored race have . . . cause for complaint . . . and I readily grant it." Again, he assumes the role of rhetorical arbiter, but in this case over "who has complaints." Lundy prophesies, however, that any attempt by Blacks to obtain their just rights by force will end in defeat and, worse, their extermination. It is in an effort to prevent this horror that he has rhetorically prophesied that "the wise and the good are now exerting themselves" (5). In this grouping of "the wise and the good," Lundy includes himself and some of the "colored people [who] have publicly condemned the pamphlet" (5). All who resist this proper, abolitionist, religious, moral, life-preserving path are only procrastinating "moral justice" and deferring "the enfranchisement of the colored race among us" (5). One might say today that they were courting political backlash. Here the plural pronoun *us* shifts back to what seems, again, an exclusively white grouping.

Both Lundy and Garrison used the black body (Walker's individual one and the collective black body) as a trope in their discourse. One reason that Garrison won out and went on to garner a larger free black following[60] may be that he understood and was sympathetic to black rage. And instead of turning the blame for it inward, on Blacks, he pointed outward to what created that rage and gave rise to it[61]—the brutalities of slavery, racial injustice, and the same yearning for revolution and freedom so well documented in the United States' own original break with England. It is, finally, these representative concerns of white American and British abolitionists, which have been under examination in this chapter, that we take into our readings of the slave testimonies to follow.

# 3. "I Know What a Slave Knows"

## Mary Prince as Witness, or the Rhetorical Uses of Experience

Oh the horrors of slavery!—How the thought of it pains my heart! But the truth ought to be told of it; and what my eyes have seen I think it is my duty to relate; for few people in England know what slavery is. I have been a slave—I have felt what a slave feels, and I know what a slave knows; and I would have all the good people in England to know it too, that they may break our chains, and set us free.

—Mary Prince, *The History of Mary Prince*

The above epigraph is arguably the most interesting and important passage in *The History of Mary Prince*. It points out Prince's need to position herself as an "authentic" eyewitness to slavery, even as her contemporary audience wants to read her as such. This passage thematizes the fact that, for Prince, the experience of slavery represents a different kind of epistemology, and that one of the crises of witnessing slavery is the very problem of how to narrate slave experience to an audience outside that epistemological community of slaves. These are the concerns I bring to this reading of Prince's *History*.

Relatively little critical commentary exists on *The History of Mary Prince: A West Indian Slave. Related by Herself.*[1] The critic primarily responsible for raising Prince from literary historical obscurity is Moira Ferguson, editor of the 1993 edition of *The History*. In her long introduction to Prince's narrative, Ferguson provides a new historicist reading of the text, which is complemented by her discussion of Prince in her book *Subject to Others*

(1992). Ferguson's reading of the narrative in these two contexts is finely wrought and compelling. She focuses, in part, on the performativity of Prince's narrative. She is especially interested in the ways in which *The History*, though an as-told-to narrative, does not

> readily surrender . . . to editorial rule. Equivocal in her [Prince's] presentation to a largely sympathetic European audience, she formulates herself as a slave-representative, as well as an individual slave-agent. For example, after warmly acknowledging the assistance of "very good" missionaries, she simultaneously inscribes the presence of an additional audience drawn from slave communities: "But [pro-slavery forces] put a cloak about the truth. It is not so. All slaves want to be free. . . . I know what slaves feel. . . . We don't mind hard work, if we had proper treatment [but] when we are quite done up, who cares for us, more than for a lame horse?"[2]

In addressing Prince's awareness of the political complexities into which her narrative intervenes, Ferguson contends that "the language of slaves markedly differs from the language of their supporters" (283). In fact, according to Ferguson, Prince speaks in a "double-voiced discourse" that addresses both her desire for manumission and her desire for narrative authority, if not autonomy (284).

Similarly, Henry Louis Gates, Jr., and William L. Andrews both comment on the extraordinary way in which Prince's text claims narrative authority for itself. Gates identifies the narrative's power and authority as deriving from its being the first published by a female slave. According to Gates, it addresses itself more specifically to the brutalities experienced by women under slavery. By assuming the position of narrator, Prince becomes the subject of narration, rather than its object:

Prince's account makes her reader acutely aware that the sexual brutalization of the black woman slave—along with the enforced severance of a mother's natural relation to her children and lover of her choice—defined more than any other aspect of slavery the daily price of her bondage. Whereas black women are objects of narration in the tales written by black men, Prince's slim yet compelling story celebrates their self-transformation into subjects, subjects as defined by those who have gained a voice.[3]

Andrews carries Gates's observation a step further, suggesting that Prince is remarkable in that she claims for herself the position of greatest authority to speak on slavery:

A black female slave [Prince] declares herself to be a more reliable authority on slavery than any white man and fully capable of speaking for all her fellow slaves, both male and female, against any white man. The implication of this declaration should not be underestimated, since it provides the first claim in the Afro-American autobiographical tradition for the black woman as singularly authorized to represent all black people, regardless of gender, in Western discourse about "what slaves feel" about the morality of slavery.[4]

This is a notable moment, since the pro-slavery advocacy's attitudes about the slave's authority to speak on matters of slavery was highly contested.

Recall the narrator's description of the character Mr. Edwards in Maria Edgeworth's "The Grateful Negro," discussed in chapter 2: "He wished that there was no such thing as slavery in the world; but he was convinced, by the arguments of *those who have the best means of obtaining information*, that the sudden emancipation of the negroes would rather increase than diminish their miseries"

(547; my italics). The "those" referred to here are not the slaves themselves. On the contrary, white men of cool reason, who can best assess the situation for the good of the slave and for the institution of slavery, are deferred to in these matters.[5] Prince's seizure of the position of narrative subject, then, coincides with or fulfills abolitionist logic that real slave experience and the literal slave body are the best proof or evidence of the brutalities of slavery. This explanation does not, however, fully account for the origin of the "authority," "self-transformation into subject," or "double-voiced discourse" attributed to Prince's narrative by Andrews, Gates, and Ferguson, respectively. To do so, it is necessary to expand the discussion beyond that of narrative strategy, to consider both the absent, real experience that the narrative represents and the way in which Prince rhetorically positions herself in relation to that experience.

A pivotal moment in the narrative, the epigraph with which I began this chapter appears in Prince's *History* just after a catalogue of injuries committed against Prince and other slaves, culminating in the particularly gruesome description of the treatment of the slave "old Daniel":

> Oh that Turk's Island was a horrible place! The people in England, I am sure, have never found out what is carried on there. Cruel, horrible place!
>
> Mr. D—— had a slave called old Daniel, whom he used to treat in the most cruel manner. Poor Daniel was lame in the hip, and could not keep up with the rest of the slaves; and our master would order him to be stripped and laid down on the ground, and have him beaten with a rod of rough briar till his skin was quite red and raw. He would then call for a bucket of salt, and fling upon the raw flesh till the man writhed on the ground like a worm, and screamed aloud with agony. This poor man's wounds were never healed, and I have often seen them

full of maggots, which increased his torments to an intolerable degree. He was an object of pity and terror to the whole gang of slaves, and in his wretched case we saw each of us, our own lot, if we should live to be as old. (64)

The story of Daniel, framed as it is by the parade of horrors narrated before it and the positioning of Daniel as a representative figure for all their fates should they live to be as old, is the perfect amalgamation of evidence for the claims Prince makes in the epigraph to this chapter.[6]

In this passage addressed expressly to the reader, Prince participates in what we might call a "politics of experience." In the same moment, she both authors and *authorizes* her speech. She is a self-appointed "expert witness" by virtue of being an "eyewitness" to the cruelties of slavery, which she knows firsthand and has up to this point been detailing. This self-positioning arises from a need to authenticate herself as narrator even as the discursive "reader"[7] both desires her authenticity and questions it. Prince confronts several rhetorical problems: How does one narrate slave experience to a readership largely ignorant of its particulars, or at least to those who do not occupy the epistemological frame of slave experience that Prince so carefully demarcates? This, of course, was a major issue for English abolitionists, because slavery was confined to the colonies and was not permitted in England. The job of convincing people in England to act against practices they did not know firsthand often required drastic measures and graphic descriptions of the horrors of slavery. These were not wanting in British anti-slavery discourse. In addition to this problem of geographical proximity, Prince identifies the problem of social location. That is, even the people of England who know of the brutalities of slavery are not themselves slaves. This is an experiential gap that only a slave can fill.

By privileging her own experience in this way, Prince's narrative also begs the question of the inaccessibility of the "real" slave experience. The best the reader can hope for is a mediated narrative, with which Prince provides the reader. The politics of experience thus functions in the narrative in multiple ways. First, it positions Prince as the authority; it legitimates her position as witness, since the reader can know slavery only through her. Second, it makes Prince's actual (or unmediated) experience into a kind of fetish object that produces and reproduces the reader's desire to know it through its ultimate unknowability. Third, it mystifies slave experience and by so doing makes Prince into a kind of channel for the reader. This discussion of access to the "real," of course, begs a more theoretical question: If Prince were to appear to the reader in person, either then or now (hypothetically, of course—through time travel, let us say), and speak to the reader personally about her story, would that change the mediated tenor of the listener's relationship to her "experience," her "testimony"?[8] It absolutely would not. Even in 1831, Prince's face-to-face testimony would present a similar set of reading challenges and be subject to the same kind of narrative scrutiny as is the text itself. The crisis of the witness, it seems, is always already a crisis of mediation. But can there ever be mediation without such crisis?

Prince positions herself as an eyewitness in this passage and gives us the ramifications of that positioning. In this sense, the politics of location, or the place from which one speaks, becomes very important. She articulates an experience that is hers alone and that is available to the readers, "the good people of England," only through her. This turns Prince's *narration* of her slave experience into the reader's experience. It is not the experience itself. Time and space erase the real experience, which leaves only the trace of its existence in the form of language. Even in the case of the eyewitness, it is a fact of language that once an experience is remembered or narrated, it is already one step removed from the "real" experience. In fact, part of the desire to bear witness, as well as the desire of the witness's audience to hear the experience, is fueled by a fetishistic desire to possess the "real" experience (the locus of *real* value), which narrative testimony can only approximate. In *Feminizing the Fetish*, Emily Apter cites the following from Karl Marx's discussion of commodity fetishism:

> Value, therefore, does not stalk about with a label describing what it is. It is value, rather, that converts every product into a social hieroglyphic. Later on, we try to decipher the hieroglyphic, to get behind the secret of our own social products; for to stamp an object of utility as a value, is just as much a social product as language. (1)

Marx's remarks are useful in accounting for the "value" of Prince's real slave experience, represented by the "social hieroglyphic" that is her narrative. Prince's very awareness of the process of witnessing, with its accompanying issues of mediation, puts her in a position to trade on her experience in a manner that authorizes her as the best person to speak about slavery.

To elaborate further this relationship between the "value" of Prince's slave experience and her claims to narrative authority, we might also look to Lindon Barrett's extremely instructive study *Blackness and Value: Seeing Double* (1999):

> The process of value attaining the condition of authority should be imagined as value blinding itself and its perceiver to its relational and disjunctive nature. . . . In authority, value contests itself in a friendly and stalemated manner. It blinds itself to the Other so as to recognize itself (by negation) in the place of the Other, effecting an acknowledgment of itself to itself.

The condition of authority—which might be called exponen-
tial value—arises when, more than violating the Other, it cites
itself in the place of the Other. Value as form (dis)figures the
Other in the images of itself. (44)

Barrett's description of the process by which value achieves authority helps us perceive even more clearly the functioning of
Prince's reversal of the epistemological terms by which she and
her contemporaries determine whose knowledge of slavery is authoritative. The rhetorical feat that Prince achieves, then, in this
process, for her purposes is not unlike the rhetorical operation
the pro-slavery advocacy had relied on for so very long to justify
and maintain their own control over how slavery and slave bodies were represented and valued. Again, to borrow Barrett's
words, "the authority of the slaveholder is fabricated and signified in the negative or, so to speak, deauthorized condition of the
African American, in this case a slave" (44).

An equally important issue to elaborate briefly here is that of
agency. I am not arguing that, in this discursive situation between
black slave and white abolitionist reader, the slave has no agency
while whites have all the agency. Rather, while white utterance
about slavery is certainly overdetermined in significant ways (dis-
cursively, when one thinks about the ongoing debates between
the pro-slavery advocacy and abolitionists or the overdeterminacy of the natural rights discourse coming out of France), it is
not the same kind of overdeterminacy to which slave narratives
are subjected. The recognition by whites of their location outside
slave experience is yet another way in which white speech about
slavery is overdetermined. Again, I do not want to equate that
with the kinds of discursive parameters placed on black speech,
because they are overdetermined in different ways. And of
course, Blacks had to be responsible to hegemonic discourses
about slave experience because white abolitionists owned the

publishing apparatuses (particularly prior to the middle of the nineteenth century) that allowed them to disseminate their discourse about slavery. Most of these early black writers understood themselves to be agentless. Consider the moment in Phillis Wheatley's "On the Death of General Wooster" (in the *Collected Works*), for example, where the appeal (even though she is speaking in the voice of Wooster) states that if America wins the revolution, its citizens will have to "let Virtue reign—And thou accord our prayers / Be victory our's, and generous freedom theirs" (lines 31–32). Mary Prince, in the epigraph to this chapter, recognizes that the power to set "us" free lies not with slaves but with the English. Even as we, in our contemporary ways, theorize and complicate the power relations that obtained between the slave and the abolitionist, we must remain cognizant of the fact that these slaves, for the most part, and even if as rhetorical strategy, understood themselves as disenfranchised and *wrote* themselves in this way.

Returning to the way in which Prince uses the fetishistic value of her narrative to create a narrative desire for the absent experience, we must recognize that the slave also becomes a consumer of the commodity fetish that the experience becomes. For instance, both Harriet Jacobs and Equiano are unable to report an event that has happened because of the sheer horror or indelicacy of it. They produce moments in the narrative when they cannot find the words to express a thing; it gets represented as inarticulable. Prince narrates one such moment early in *The History*, on the occasion of being sold away from her family:

> Oh dear! *I cannot bear to think of that day,*—it is too much.—It recalls the great grief that passed to and fro through my mind, whilst listening to the pitiful words of my poor mother, weeping for the loss of her children. *I wish I could find words to tell you all I then felt and suffered.* (51; my emphasis)

In these moments of unspeakable horror, the narrative is denied to us and is reduced to the sheer personal memory of the witness, which we can witness only as that which is unspeakable. In this way, the testimony creates an even stronger desire on the part of the reader for the thing that is unspeakable by the witness. We witness, in effect, the performance of the inability to bear witness.

The slave's inability or unwillingness to report such horrible events may also derive from an awareness of texts in circulation during the late eighteenth and early nineteenth centuries that discussed the brutalities of slavery in particular and graphic terms. I think here especially of Thomas Clarkson's *History of the Rise, Progress, and Accomplishment of the Abolition of the African Slave Trade by the British Parliament*. The rhetorical gesture of unspeakability is, in part, effective because those kinds of horrific images are already part of public discourse. It also has to do with geography. In the case of both Jacobs and Prince, we are dealing with audiences (white Northerners and the English, respectively) who are one step removed from slave experience itself. Unlike Southerners or West Indian planters (those, at least, who were not absentee landlords), many of these readers would not have had firsthand experience with slavery. It was not in their backyards or a part of their daily lives. As a result, many were personally unaware of the horrific tortures and details of the peculiar institution. The rhetorical gesture of unspeakability is enabled by geography because the thing that is unknowable becomes hyperunknowable. If the testimony already exists at the level of that which is unknowable, the real experience that the narrator represents as unspeakable horror becomes doubly unknowable, and the desire for the absence it represents is almost insatiable.

Note that Prince identifies her desire to witness as a "duty." The sense of the "duty" to relate is somewhat different from the idea of the "desire" to bear witness. They participate in a different politics. Desire suggests less urgency than does duty. Duty is something that one feels compelled to do, for reasons that are larger than the individual or that exceed the individual drive or desire. After all, the desire for such testimony is well documented: the hearings held by Parliament in which testimony was given by whites of what they had observed in the West Indies; the public testimonials organized by abolitionists, where former slaves gave their testimonies; comments like that of Margaret Fuller about Douglass's narrative, "It is an excellent piece of writing and on that score to be prized as a specimen of the powers of the black race. . . . We prize highly all such evidence of this kind";[9] and, finally, the appeal to the marked slave body for the indelible trace of slavery, as in the case of Mary Prince's scars. All these attest to the desire for the real, original, authentic slave experience. Since the experience of slavery itself is inaccessible to nonslaves, the rhetoric of authenticity, which pervades the slavery debates, requires witnesses and testimony that approximate the value of that irretrievable experience. Put another way, it takes a witness for the "truth" to be told; hence the fetishistic value of Prince's slave experience.

The opening statement of the "Preface" to Prince's narrative, by Thomas Pringle, Prince's editor, identifies the desire to bear witness as arising first and foremost from Prince herself:

> The idea of writing Mary Prince's history was first suggested by herself. She wished it to be done, she said, that good people in England might hear from a slave what a slave had felt and suffered; and a letter of her late master's, which will be found in the Supplement, induced me to accede to her wish without further delay. (45)

Pringle here refutes the pro-slavery advocacy claims that slave narratives were instruments manufactured by the Anti-Slavery

Society. More important, Pringle reinforces the idea that Prince's testimony is an authentic representation of slavery because it comes from a slave. Thus, he himself bears witness to Prince's politics of experience. Pringle's description of the editorial process for the narrative elaborates his anticipation of the doubts that will be cast on its authenticity. Such narrative details themselves, both in the text and in the supplemental materials accompanying the narrative, assume important evidentiary status. These details identify the testimonial quality of the narrative, even as they demarcate the text as a site of contestation.

The extent to which such real slave experience becomes the "value" behind the "social hieroglyphic" that is the narrative itself must not be underestimated; nor should the necessity to demonstrate the utter authenticity of the narrative account. By authenticity here I mean, specifically, the extent to which the narrative appeals to a "verifiable,"[10] real slave experience, without artifice or editorial affectation. Consider the caveat to the reader at the close of Pringle's preface to the narrative:

> I shall here merely notice further, that the Anti-Slavery Society have no concern whatever with this publication, nor are they in any degree responsible for the statements it contains. I have published the tract, not as their Secretary, but in my private capacity; and any profits that may arise from the sale will be exclusively appropriated to the benefit of Mary Prince herself. (46)

The narrative style had to perform simplicity, artlessness, and truth in its accounting of the brutalities of slavery. This explains why slave narratives, such as those of Jacobs and Equiano, for example, frequently begin by asserting that they are giving us the veritable "round unvarnish'd tale."[11] James Olney gives extended attention to this process of authentication in the slave narrative.

He also addresses the comparison, often drawn by abolitionists and reviewers of slave narratives, between the slave narrator and Shakespeare's Othello. Commenting on the rigor and regimen of the slave narrative's order of narration, he offers advice so useful that I may be forgiven for quoting him at some length:

Of the kind of memory central to the act of autobiography . . . Ernest Cassirer has written: "Symbolic memory is the process by which man not only repeats his past experience but also reconstructs this experience. Imagination becomes a necessary element of true recollection." In that word "imagination," however, lies the joker for an ex-slave who would write the narrative of his life in slavery. What we find Augustine doing in Book X of the *Confessions*—offering up a disquisition on memory that makes both memory itself and the narrative that it surrounds fully symbolic—would be inconceivable in a slave narrative. Of course ex-slaves do exercise memory in their narratives, but they never talk about it as Augustine does, as Rousseau does, as Wordsworth does . . . as a hundred other autobiographers (not to say novelists like Proust) do. Ex-slaves *cannot* talk about it because of the premise that there is nothing doubtful or mysterious about memory; on the contrary, it is assumed to be a clear, unfailing record of events sharp and distinct that need only to be transformed into descriptive language to become the sequential narrative of a life in slavery. In the same way, the ex-slave writing his narrative cannot afford to put the present in conjunction with the past . . . for fear that in so doing he will appear, from the present, to be reshaping and so distorting and falsifying the past. As a result, the slave narrative is most often a non-memorial description fitted to a preformed mold, a mold with regular depressions here and equally regular prominences there—virtually obligatory figures, scenes, turns of phrase, observances, and authentications

—that carry over from narrative to narrative and give to them as a group the species character that we designate by the phrase "slave narrative." (150–51)

And indeed, Prince, on several occasions in *The History*, describes or mentions being beaten or witnessing the beatings of fellow slaves. These instances of brutality are corroborated by her editor through a literal return to the site of Prince's body. The marks on her body—themselves the trace or residue of slavery's brutality—become the last authentic, irreducible, material sign of the truth of her narrative. Her scarred, black body—unlike language and rhetoric—cannot but tell the truth. In the absence of the real, unmediated slave experience—which, as I have said, is impossible to access—the closest one can hope to come to that real experience is Prince's black body: the very palimpsest upon which slave experience is indelibly written for all to read.

Prince's body quite literally assumes evidentiary status. In the third appendix to *The History*, the editor presents a letter authored by his wife, Mrs. Pringle, to a Mrs. Townsend of the Birmingham Ladies' Society for the Relief of Negro Slaves. We are told that Mrs. Townsend, like many others, made inquiries "respecting the existence of marks of severe punishment on Mary Prince's body" (119). To this request for such incontrovertible evidence of the horrors of slavery, Mrs. Pringle responds by letter to Mrs. Townsend in this manner:

> My husband having read to me the passage in your last letter to him, expressing a desire to be furnished with some description of the marks of former ill-usage on Mary Prince's person,—I beg in reply to state, that the whole of the back part of her body is distinctly scarred, and, as it were, *chequered*, with the vestiges of severe floggings. Besides this, there are many large scars on other parts of her person, exhibiting an appearance as if the

flesh had been deeply cut or lacerated with gashes, by some in-
strument wielded by most unmerciful hands. Mary affirms,
that all these scars were occasioned by various cruel punishments she had mentioned or referred to in her narrative; and
of the entire truth of this statement I have no hesitation in de-
claring myself perfectly satisfied, not only from my depend-
ence on her uniform capacity, but also from my previous observation of similar cases at the Cape of Good Hope.

In order to put you in possession of such full and authentic
evidence, respecting the marks on Mary Prince's person, as
may serve your benevolent purpose in making the inquiry, I
beg to add to my own testimony that of Miss Strickland (the
lady who wrote down in this house the narratives of Mary
Prince and Ashton Warner), together with the testimonies of
my sister Susan and my friend Miss Browne—all of whom were
present and assisted me this day in a second inspection of
Mary's body. (119–20)

The letter is then signed by each of the women present. This letter is telling for the confluence of discourses in it. There is the
quasi-medical/scientific language used to describe the "inspection" of Prince's body, which lends clinical authority to the
women's examination. The episode also is both understood and
written as a "legal" event. Mrs. Pringle begs to add to her own
"testimony" that of the women who accompanied her in inspect-
ing Prince. She further signals her reader as to the purpose of
these corroborating witnesses. They are to put Mrs. Townsend
(and, by extension, anyone else under whose gaze this letter
might fall, as it understands itself as a private document that is to
be used publicly) "in possession of . . . full and authentic evidence" about Prince's body. Lest someone charge Mrs. Pringle
singularly with misreading Prince's scarred body, she employs a
core of readers who corroborate her reading of Prince's body.

I close this chapter by briefly discussing the conclusion of *The History*. In the last few pages of the narrative, Prince again —this time with the force and benefit of the various experiences she has related—reasserts her position as an expert and most reliable witness to slavery by virtue of her former slave identity and slave experience:

> I am often much vexed, and I feel great sorrow when I hear some people in this country say, that the slaves do not need better usage, and do not want to be free. They believe the foreign people, who deceive them, and say slaves are happy. I say, Not so. How can slaves be happy when they have the halter round their neck and the whip upon their back? . . . There is no modesty or decency shown by the owner to his slaves. . . . Since I have been here [in England] I have often wondered how English people can go out into the West Indies and act in such a beastly manner. But when they go to the West Indies, they forget God and all feeling of shame, I think, since they can see and do such things. (83)

The effect of Prince's self-assertion at this point is even clearer and more dramatic. She explicitly links her self-declaration as subject of her testimony to her anti-slavery views. She declares explicitly that her insight is better than that of any of the English when she corrects the misconception that slaves do not want to be free with the statement beginning, "I say, Not so." This assertion of the willful "I" should not be underestimated. Indeed, this corrective and willful "I" is the same one who speaks these telling words:

> Yet they [West Indian planters] come home and say, and make some good people believe, that slaves don't want to get out of slavery. But they put a cloak about the truth. It is not so. All

slaves want to be free—to be free is very sweet. I will say the truth to English people who may read this history . . . I have been a slave myself—I know what slaves feel—I can tell by myself what other slaves feel, and by what they have told me. The man that says slaves be quite happy in slavery—that they don't want to be free—that man is either ignorant or a lying person. I never heard a slave say so. I never heard a Buckra man say so, till I heard tell of it in England. (84)

Here, Prince completely reverses the established roles ascribed to slave and master. In her logic, the slave knows best what the slave wants. That she declares she "will say the truth to English people," as opposed to the lies that have been told by the planters, is a bold move in itself. And to correct "the man that says slaves be quite happy in slavery" by using slave testimony (which, ironically enough, would have been a legal impossibility in Prince's West Indies, since black testimony against whites was not admissible in West Indian courts) is also a radical gesture. Prince's declaration that she knows what a slave feels echoes the earlier statement made in the epigraph to this chapter. Here, she does not simply represent all slaves, as she does in the earlier instance; rather, slave experience itself is universalized in Prince's rhetoric, to the point where she declares, "I can tell by myself what other slaves feel, and by what they have told me." The representative position Prince occupies becomes absolute. "By myself" in this context must be read to signify as "from my own experience," as it is opposed to those experiences that other slaves have related to her.

Hence, real slave experience not only makes Prince's word the best word but has a far broader, democratizing effect. All slaves can and do know what she knows and have access to that real truth. This truth, as it is described here by Prince, is a truth that circulates primarily in the slave community. That is, she not only has access to real slave experience, which qualifies her as the most reliable witness, but she also has access to the experiences of other slaves, who share their experiences with her. Ultimately, Prince's truth derives its value from the fetishization of real slave experience and a cultural essentialism that trades on being inside the slave community, as opposed to those who can speak only from the outside. The result is a reversal of the dominant rhetorical logic. Instead of others knowing what is best for the slave, for Prince the slave is always in the best position to witness slavery, and all outsiders are compelled to look to him or her if they would know the "truth" of the peculiar institution.

# 4. Appropriating the Word

## Phillis Wheatley, Religious Rhetoric, and the Poetics of Liberation

Remember, Christians, Negros black as Cain,
May be refin'd, and join th'angelic train.

—Phillis Wheatley

While I was thus employed by my master, I was often a witness to cruelties of every kind, which were exercised on my unhappy fellowslaves.

—Olaudah Equiano

This chapter is an investigation of the function and circulation of religious rhetoric in the poetry and letters of Phillis Wheatley. It is particularly concerned with the rhetorical strategies that she employed to bear witness to slavery in the late eighteenth century (the earliest context for institutional abolitionism). Through her oppositional discourse on Christianity, she anticipated the moral arguments of pro-slavers, especially in her characterizations of the Christian God. A close examination of specific testimonial moments[1] in her writings demonstrates that while Wheatley knows and rehearses Enlightenment discourses on natural rights quite fluently, her resistance to slavery is coded in her figurative, poetic language.

Much of the critical response to the work of Phillis Wheatley has ignored its literary substance. The record of Wheatley criticism, from her contemporaries to the present, reads more like a sociological graph of changing racial attitudes than like a critical history. We can only imagine that, had Wheatley been able to anticipate the lack of literary substance in the debate the academy and literati would wage around her work or the seeming lack of compassion, appreciation, and understanding that later critics would have for her sociohistorical context and its inevitable impact on her public writings, she might have risked even more than she did or, in the worst possible case, aborted her ostensibly impossible task all together.

To take but a few examples: Seymour Gross in 1966 described her work with "this Negro poetess so well fits the Uncle Tom syndrome . . ."[2] Earlier, in 1939, J. Saunders Redding charged that "it is this negative, bloodless, unracial quality in Phillis Wheatley that makes her seem superficial, especially to members of her own race."[3] By the mid-1970s, so much of this pernicious and painfully ahistorical criticism had been written that by way of summation of these critics in his book *Phillis Wheatley in the Black American Beginnings*, William Robinson wrote, "Most condemnatory are some modern Blacks who dismiss Phillis out of hand as 'an early Boston Aunt Jemima,' 'a colonial handkerchief head,' 'utterly irrelevant to the identification and liberation of the Black man.'"[4]

Some more recent critical voices have done much to expand the idea of the significance of Wheatley's historical context on her literary work.[5] The work of these scholars is to be lauded since, as the critical-historical record of Wheatley has borne out, it is scarcely possible to analyze her work fruitfully in a purely formalist critique, without attention to context. And of course, any attention to context in the work of Phillis Wheatley necessitates an engagement with the circumstances of the work's production. What remains, it seems, is for critics actually to read Wheatley's poetry with this attention to history in mind. In general, the criticism on Wheatley tends to analyze the significance of the idea of a Phillis Wheatley in larger discussions about African humanity (Gates), slavery and abolitionism (nearly everyone), entrance

into the public sphere (Nott), or her inclusion in—or role as progenitor of—the black canon (Reid-Pharr), while doing little to
address and to examine the writing itself. To be at its best, Wheatley scholarship must come to do both. That is, we must be attentive to historical context and to the larger intellectual debates
and discourses in which Phillis Wheatley becomes enlisted
(which much of the recent criticism does), at the same time
using sustained internal evidence from her writing itself to make
our critical claims. There have been a few recent notable excep-
tions; Hilene Flanzbaum's 1993 essay, "Unprecedented Liberties: Re-reading Phillis Wheatley" strikes me as exemplary in this
regard. Still, more attention to this matter of locating points of
genuine connection between the attention to Wheatley's historical context and an actual examination of her writing is much
warranted in Wheatley criticism. For these reasons, I find it appropriate to add to the current scholarship my own historical investigation of the context from which Wheatley framed her poetical works and their social and political significance. Specifically, I consider the role Christianity plays in Wheatley's poetics
of resistance to slavery.

The young African girl whom we know as Phillis Wheatley was
born probably around 1753, somewhere in present Senegal or
Gambia. In 1761, the little eight-year-old African girl was cap-
tured and brought to Boston as a slave. Poorly clad, young, weak,
and rather sickly, it was not expected that she would bring a
"good price." So when John Wheatley and his wife, Susannah, decided to purchase the girl, the merchant was more than fair
about the negotiations.[6]

It was good fortune that brought young Phillis into the home,
lives, and care of the benevolent Wheatleys, where she was
treated more like a member of the family than a domestic slave.
Mrs. Wheatley was particularly enamored by the small, frail child
and took a keen interest in her intellectual development and

physical and emotional care. Phillis's education began when Mrs. Wheatley noticed her trying to form letters on the wall. Recognizing her uncommon intellectual potential, the Wheatleys began teaching her English. Mrs. Wheatley's daughter Mary became an active participant in this endeavor. Serving as Phillis's tutor, Mary taught the little girl to read and write.[7]

Phillis developed quickly, as she had a very healthy appetite for learning. She studied the Bible, astronomy, ancient history, and English and Latin literature.[8] She was almost completely literate after sixteen months of tutoring. So impressive was her progress that the literati and others of high stature in her society began to take notice of her. In fact, on December 21, 1767, at the age of fourteen, Phillis published her first poem, "On Messrs. Hussey and Coffin," in the Newport, Rhode Island *Mercury*.[9] This was not, however, the work that established the international reputation that Phillis Wheatley would come to know during her life. This did not occur until 1771 (she had continued writing verse since her first publication), when Phillis, first on broadsides and later in journals, published her most celebrated piece, "On the Death of the Rev. Mr. George Whitefield.—1770." Whitefield was a popular evangelist who preached throughout the American colonies and was considered a friend to American Blacks. He was also the chaplin to the countess of Huntingdon (a patron of Phillis's, to whom she would later dedicate her first published volume of verse).[10] The publication of this poem solidly established the name of Phillis Wheatley in America and in England. Phillis most enjoyed, and her poems seemed to be most influenced by, the works of John Milton and Alexander Pope, an assertion borne out in the meter (iambic pentameter) and the use of the neoclassical heroic couplet in her poetry.[11]

There is a strong tendency on the part of some contemporary readers of Wheatley to romanticize the time period during which this young adult poet lived or to view her existence as idyllic. Phillis Wheatley came of age and was educated in an America greatly under the influence of the Enlightenment, or the "Age of Reason." As a movement, the Enlightenment attempted to liberate humankind from the restraints of unexamined authority, religion, and prejudice through "right reason." These are noble goals, indeed. It does not follow, however, that the Enlightenment necessarily reasoned "rightly" on issues of race, gender, class, and the like. In fact, some of the great philosophers of the time, among them David Hume and Immanuel Kant, argued that Blacks were slaves because it was impossible for them to reason. Though the discourse of "natural rights" dominated such philosophical inquiry, one of the main questions of the day was whether these rights extended to all people equally, without regard to hierarchies (Blacks, women, the poor and unpropertied, etc.). Henry Louis Gates, Jr., best characterizes the effect the Enlightenment had on Blacks:

> Writing [in the Enlightenment] . . . was taken to be the visible sign of reason. Blacks were "reasonable," and hence "men," if—and only if—they demonstrated mastery of "the arts and sciences," the eighteenth century's formula for writing. So, while the Enlightenment is characterized by its foundation on man's ability to reason, it simultaneously used the absence and presence of reason to delimit and circumscribe the very humanity of the cultures and people of color which Europeans had been "discovering" since the Renaissance. The urge toward the systematization of all human knowledge (by which we characterize the Enlightenment) led to the relegation of black people to a lower place in the great chain of being, an ancient construct that arranged all of creation on a vertical scale from plants, insects, and animals through man to the angels and God himself.[12]

The predominant belief about Blacks during the Enlightenment was that they were incapable of reason, that they were not of the same variety of humanity as whites, and that they were therefore suited to the condition of slavery. Philosophers as different in their views as Kant, in *Anthropology from a Pragmatic Point of View;* Hume, in "Of National Characters"; and Hegel, in *The Philosophy of History* and elsewhere, all schematized the relations among the races. In all these cases, Africans were placed at the bottom.

This mode of thought was perpetuated in the local colonial churches, especially in the South (where Blacks often attended in reserved sections), through politicized and what we today would call fundamentalist readings of biblical scriptures. On any given Sabbath in these church services, one might hear "thus says the Lord" to the slaves:

> Servants,[13] be obedient to them that are your masters according to the flesh, with fear and trembling, in singleness of your heart as unto Christ.          —Eph. 6:5, King James Version

> Exhort servants to be obedient unto their own masters, and to please them well in all things.
> —Titus 2:9, King James Version

> Servants, be subject to your masters with all fear; not only to the good and gentle, but also to the froward.
> —1 Peter 2:18, King James Version

These most oppressive appropriations of the scriptures, and by extension, of the slaves' loyalty to God, were very useful to the slaveholder in maintaining psychological control over his servants.[14]

While Wheatley was well received by many of high stature during her lifetime, those same people often saw Wheatley as a threat. This was not because her poetry was openly political, nor simply because she was a poet. That she was a black, female poet, however, posed some challenges to the reigning thought of her day on the humanity of the African. Her mere existence aroused the latent fears of the white intelligentsia. Given the prevailing thought about Blacks during the Enlightenment, especially during the height of commerce (and by extension, the height of the slave trade), Wheatley's very life as a literary figure could be read as a profound resistance to oppression. She undercut the myth that Africans could not write, could not master the arts and sciences, and could not reason. Although many tried to claim that Wheatley was an exception among Blacks, she remained proof positive to America and to the world that any black, given the advantages that she had been given, could succeed. Wheatley's existence was unsettling for the white mind in large measure because it compelled whites to confront the moral possibility that Africans were not innately inferior.

Considering the philosophical racism of the Enlightenment, white paranoia about literate Blacks, the white racist practices of Christianity, a white racist press, and the lack of a black community to support her,[15] it is a miracle that Phillis Wheatley could find within herself the resolve to write. It is a tribute both to her intelligence and to her commitment to ameliorating the condition of her people that she was able to politicize her writing in the way that she did for a primarily white, Christian, and racist audience.

Phillis Wheatley's story is one of the making of a poet in spite of the odds. She wrote in spite of the fact that her work had to meet with the approval of white publishers and patrons.[16] She wrote in spite of the fact that she was tokenized. She wrote even in spite of the fact that she had to go to London in 1773 to be published (this won her the distinction of being the first black American to publish a book)[17] because no one in America was willing to print her work.[18] As we take a closer look at Wheatley's poetical works and letters, it is imperative to keep in mind the brief contextual sketch in which we have located her.

Critics of the twentieth century, especially those of the earlier part of the century, have been relentless in their condemnation of Wheatley for her perceived lack of racial solidarity. Redding says of her:

> Judged in the light of the day in which she wrote, judged by that day's standards and accomplishments, she was an important poet. As a Negro poet she stands out remarkably, for her work lacks the characteristics of thought one would expect to find.[19]

The key phrases here are "judged in the light of the day" and "expect to find." It is less than clear what Redding means by "the light of the day." Redding obviously assumes a very different context than do I. Exactly what, then, was it that Redding and his cohorts were "expecting" to find in the literature of a black, female slave writing before the Revolutionary War in America? What were their expectations of the first black woman to be published in the English language? This question of expectation shapes their focus: Was Wheatley's poetry "black" enough (which in itself is a problematic measure of critical assessment)? After Redding's denigrating reading of Wheatley in *To Make a Poet Black*, he compares both her and Jupiter Hammon (who wrote a short slave pamphlet in 1760)[20] to George Moses Horton:

> What Hammon lacked in audacity and color and what Miss Wheatley failed to show in enthusiasm and racial kinship is more than supplied by George Moses Horton. If the former were motivated only by an aimless urge to write, finding as they went along, willy-nilly, ideas, emotions, and thoughts to give expression to, Horton started from an emotional basis. He first

wanted to say something. Hammon and Miss Wheatley were negative; Horton was positive. He felt, albeit selfishly, the motivation derived from the Negro's position in America. He felt too something of the wonder and mystery, the tragic beauty, and the pathetic ugliness of life. Above-all, he had the gift of laughter. He was the first "natural-born" poet of the Negro race in America.[21]

There are some fundamental problems with the line of argument Redding uses against Wheatley and Hammon. These problems are illustrative of the characteristics that dominated critical discussion of early African American texts up until the last two decades of the twentieth century. First, Redding imposes a self-created, universal construct on the works of all these writers, based on the fact that they were all black. In so doing, he ignores their differing historical contexts, thus dehistoricizing their work to a point where little of critical value can be said about them.

Consider that Hammon was first published in 1760, Wheatley (as an adult) in 1771. Horton was not born until 1797 (thirteen years after Wheatley's death) and was not published until 1829, fifty-five years after Wheatley's first volume was published. To take seriously Redding's argument that Horton was the first "natural-born" poet of the Negro race, we would have to believe that the sociohistorical circumstances for Blacks in America remained unaltered for over a half century. Of course, this is not the case. In that fifty-year period, the abolitionist movement (as discussed in chapter 2) grew tremendously; the number of free blacks was on the rise; and the black press became a reality. What did this mean for black people writing during the time that Horton wrote? Robinson says it best:

It was not until the 19th century, with the founding of the Negro press in John Russwurm's "Freedom Journal" (1828) [two

years before Horton was published], that Blacks found publishing outlets for their more freely acknowledged protests.[22]

Wheatley too found outlets in her poetry to express her views
on issues of black subjugation and oppression. Context, however,
demanded that her approach be unique, tailored for her predominantly white audience through the use of Christianity as an
audience identifier or "common denominator" and written to at-
tain publication in the white colonial press. Had Wheatley's writing contained what Redding "expected to find," it might never
have found its way into print, and the name Phillis Wheatley
would have disappeared in the annals of history with other unpublished black writers.

Having discussed the terms under which Wheatley wrote, I
now turn to some of the basic themes and poetic devices that
Wheatley employed in her work, in order to assess her contribution to abolitionist discourse. Consider one of the original poems
published in the 1773 collection, "To the University of Cambridge in New-England." The poem was actually composed in
1767, when Wheatley was about thirteen years old. The first
stanza reads:

> While an intrinsic ardor prompts to write,
> The Muses promise to assist my pen.
> 'Twas not long since I left my native shore,
> The land of errors and Egyptian gloom:
> Father of mercy! 'twas thy gracious hand
> Brought me in safety from those dark abodes.[23]

In the first two lines of this poem, Wheatley tells us whence her
desire to write poetry comes. She tells us rather explicitly in the
first line of the poem that it is "an intrinsic ardor" that prompts
her to write. As June Jordan observes, "It was she who created

herself a poet, notwithstanding and in despite of everything around her."[24] Some critics argue that Wheatley's references to Africa in the first stanza as "the land of errors and Egyptian gloom" (line 4) and to "dark abodes" (line 6) testify to the poet's disdain for her native land. This reading of the line is facile and is not supported by the body of Wheatley's work. Wheatley does not hate Africa; she hates "pagan" or "Egyptian" Africa. It is consistently evident throughout her poetry that she considers Christianity the most important thing in her life. This explains why she prefers Christian America (the common denominator between her and her white audience) to pagan Africa. In a sense, Wheatley, as slave witness, appropriates "the word" of Christianity as a vehicle to empower her own very important message, namely, that Blacks have reason, in much the same way that whites used "the word" to oppress the slaves. The way in which Wheatley masters this approach is shown more clearly in another of her published works, "On Being Brought from Africa to America."

In the first line of "On Being Brought from Africa to America," Wheatley refers to Africa as a "pagan land": "'Twas mercy brought me from my *Pagan* land." Her criticism here is directed not against Africa but rather against the ignorance of the Christian God that, to her mind, plagues the continent. Wheatley then makes a subtle political statement on the racism of American society: "Some view our sable race with scornful eye" (5). After quoting what was probably the representative sentiment of whites at the time ("Their color is a diabolic die" [6]), she addresses—indeed, interpellates—the readers as "Christians" and cautions them against such non-Christian views of the Negro: "Remember, *Christians, Negros* black as Cain / May be refined, and join the angelic train" (lines 7–8). Notice once again how Wheatley opens the poem with her testimony, tactically privileging her Christian identity. Next, she critiques her society. And then, she warns the Christian reader of his or her moral responsibility to acknowledge her equality.

The symmetrical structure of the poem is also significant. The poem divides naturally into two halves in terms of its punctuation and its shift in subject. The first four lines comment on the mercy that brought Wheatley from Africa to America, where she eventually came to know the Christian God. It is not surprising that Wheatley can look at her transition from Africa to America as an act of mercy, since to her it effects her redemption. Lest we think she also views her change in social position from freedom to slavery in America as an act of mercy, Wheatley addresses white racism head on in the second half of the poem: "Some view our sable race with scornful eye, / 'Their color is a diabolic die.' / Remember, *Christians*, *Negros* black as Cain, / May be refin'd, and join th'angelic train." Thus, in the very structure of the poem, Wheatley separates the two issues that are so easily conflated by some of her readers, that is, her gratitude for redemption as opposed to her condemnation of slavery. Too often the former has been incorrectly thought to deny the latter.

Wheatley utilizes the rhetoric of Christianity even more radically in the poem "On the Death of the Rev. Mr George Whitefield.—1770." The very act of choosing to write a poem on Whitefield is a political statement, since he was known in colonial America and in England as a friend to the African. The strong Christian tone of the poem attests to Wheatley's pious nature. The first twenty-seven lines describe Whitefield's life as a servant to God. Yet Wheatley's own rhetoric of racial liberation appears in what are supposedly words from a Whitefield sermon in the poem:

> *"Take him, my dear Americans, he said,*
> *"Be your complaints on his kind bosom laid:*
> *"Take him, ye Africans, he longs for you;*

"*Impartial Savior is his title due:*
"*Washed in the fountain of redeeming blood,*
"*You shall be sons, and kings and priests to God.*"[25]
(lines 32–37)

The possibilities for reading this poem become even more interesting, as it exists in two variant versions beyond this one. Either Wheatley edited copies of the poem before arriving at the above 1773 edition version, which was more palatable to her white readership, or her publishers made the changes in the lines before they went to press. There is no conclusive evidence one way or the other. The variants of these lines read thus:

*Take HIM ye Africans, he longs for you;*
*Impartial SAVIOUR, is his title due;*
*If you will chuse [sic] to walk in grace's road,*
*You shall be sons, and kings, and priests to God.*
　　　　　　　　　—*First Version*

*Take him, ye Africans, he longs for you,*
*Impartial Saviour is his Title due.*
*If you will walk in Grace's heavenly Road,*
*He'll make you free, and Kings, and Priests to God.*
　　　　　　　　　—*Second Version*

There is, of course, a notable difference between the second variant of the poem and the printed version in the 1773 edition of *Poems.* The former implicitly represents Enlightenment whites as morally wrong on the issue of slavery. Stating the words "He'll make you free" carries implications for a white, Enlightenment readership that it neither wanted nor was prepared to receive. Even as the words appeared in the 1773 publication, however, "Impartial Saviour" would have been considered a radical gesture, since it implies a critique of the great chain of being and questions the concept of a hierarchy of persons under God.[26]

Wheatley critic John Shields develops a similar reading of Wheatley's poem "On the Death of General Wooster."[27] He suggests that Wheatley's political concerns are not always for the Christian common good but at times specifically speak for her fellow Blacks who are still in bondage. Embedded in this poem, once again, is an appeal that the freedom of black people accompany the colonies' pursuit of freedom. Wheatley tactically attributes to the deceased General Wooster the following prayer in the poem:

> *But how presumptuous shall we hope to find*
> *Divine acceptance with th'Almighty mind—*
> *While yet (O deed Ungenerous!) they disgrace*
> *And hold in bondage Afric's blameless race?*
> *Let Virtue reign—And thou accord our prayers*
> *Be victory our's, and generous freedom theirs.*
> (lines 27–32)

As in "On the Death of the Rev. Mr. George Whitefield," Wheatley speaks through the prophetic and critical voice of a dead, white, male body her own most radical words of liberation. This ventriloquism is an interesting reversal of the theatrical and discursive use of the black, slave body in abolitionist discourse, outlined in chapter 1. Shields contends that Wheatley here marks the contradiction between what Christianity professes—brotherhood—and what Christianity does—slavery. Wheatley calls Blacks the "blameless race" and slavery "ungenerous." She holds that if virtue reigns and America is victorious over Britain, then Blacks should receive "generous freedom" as well.

I consider one more rhetorical strategy that Wheatley uses to witness slavery. In her polemic against slavery, Wheatley turns the rhetoric of the Enlightenment back upon itself. She becomes a master of the very language of "reason" that is, arguably, one of the most potent vehicles of racial oppression. In a letter to the Reverend Samuel Hopkins about two Negroes who "are desirous of returning to their native country. [*sic*] to preach the gospel," Wheatley writes:

> Methinks, Rev. Sir, this is the beginning of that happy period foretold by the Prophets, when all shall know the Lord from the least to the greatest, and that without the assistance of *human Art of Eloquence.* (my emphasis)[28]

This statement aptly illustrates Wheatley's awareness of the power of rhetoric and of language. Moreover, it reveals a certain distrust of rhetoric, given her belief in God's ability to accomplish the work of spreading the gospel without the use of "Eloquence." Her sensitivity to rhetoric or eloquence is not surprising, given how much a part of the colonial idiom persuasive rhetoric was (e.g., pamphleteering, public debates, speechmaking, epistolary writings, etc.).

While Wheatley here expresses a distrust of rhetoric, she nonetheless understands the pragmatic necessity of using it to advance her own politics. In her most interesting epistle, to Samson Occom, Wheatley appropriates the language of the Enlightenment for her own subversive discourse, rendering ironic the very trope of "reason":

> I have just this Day received your obliging kind Epistle, and am greatly satisfied with your *Reasons* respecting the Negroes, and think highly *reasonable* what you offer in Vindication of their *natural Rights:* Those that invade them cannot be insensible that the *divine Light* is chasing away the *thick Darkness* which broods over the land of Africa; and the *Chaos* which has

reigned so long, is converting into *beautiful Order*, and reveals more and more clearly, the glorious Dispensation of *civil and religious Liberty*, which are so inseparably united, that there is little or no Enjoyment of the one without the other. . . . God grants Deliverance in his own way and Time, and get him honor upon all those whose Avarice impels them to countenance and help forward the Calamities of their Fellow Creatures. This I desire not for their Hurt, but to convince them of the strange Absurdity of their Conduct whose *Words and Actions are so diametrically opposite.* How well the Cry for Liberty, and the reverse Disposition for the Exercise of oppressive Power over others agree,—I humbly think it does not require the *Penetration of a Philosopher to determine.* (my emphasis)[29]

Whom is Wheatley addressing in this letter? Occom was an educated Native American who, as an envoy to the earl of Dartmouth, was largely responsible for founding Dartmouth College, where Native Americans and Africans for a short time were permitted to attend. Judging from the relative candidness of her letters to Obour Tanner and to Occum, Wheatley was more forthcoming in her correspondence with them than in communications with whites. Note her use of the term *reason* and its derivation *reasonable* in such close proximity to each other to modify Occum, a Native American. Here, Wheatley appropriates and turns ironic the trope of "reason," in an eighteenth-century context in which Native Americans (the "noble savages") figured just above Africans on the great chain of being. Wheatley's use of the binary "light" and "dark" (which commonly connoted good and evil, especially in Christian symbolism) is significant, since this letter was also intended for a white readership.[30] The same is true of the image of chaos turning into "beautiful Order" (another important theme of the Enlightenment). These images function early in the letter to draw the reader into an immediate compliance with the author, before she makes the liberationist "turn" that soon follows. This discursive strategy occurs repeatedly in Wheatley's poetry and prose. In the latter part of the letter, Wheatley comments on the flagrant contradictions in contemporary religious and political rhetoric: "This I desire not for their Hurt, but to convince them of the strange Absurdity of their Conduct whose Words and Actions are so diametrically opposite." She thus condemns a contemporary rhetoric that has trickery, deception, and in this case oppression as its goal.

The final critical gesture that Wheatley makes in this epistle, and arguably the most poignant, is found in the statement that it does not take the "Penetration of a Philosopher" to discern how closely aligned are the "Cry for Liberty" and the "Exercise of oppressive Power over others." Combining a sardonic tone with a powerful rhetorical thrust, Wheatley in one critical gesture manages to debunk—or at least to problematize—the privileged category of "reason," which is signified in the phrase "Penetration of a Philosopher." This letter clearly documents Wheatley's seriousness of purpose and her intense awareness of the political stakes, not only of her work and her words but of her very existence as an educated African slave woman in a racist, sexist, Enlightenment world.

# 5. Speaking as "the African"

## Olaudah Equiano's Moral Argument against Slavery

While engaged with many of the same Enlightenment discourses as Wheatley's poems, *The Interesting Narrative of the Life of Olaudah Equiano, or Gustavus Vassa, the African. Written by Himself*[1] makes use of a significantly different politics. Equiano marshals the army of contemporary metaphors at his disposal to make a highly articulate argument against slavery on the basis of Christian morality. In so doing, he weaves a discourse as compelling as any philosophical discourse of his day. His approach has the dual effect of disputing the moral arguments in favor of slavery and serving to demonstrate his own humanity by adopting the cultural pose of philosopher and saint. Indeed, Equiano's narrative goes so far as to suggest the moral superiority of people of color over whites (an idea that would not achieve fullest articulation until over forty years later, with the publication of David Walker's *Appeal* in 1831).

While most critics of Equiano tend to conflate the distinction between Equiano the author of the narrative and Equiano the subject of the narrative, my reading focuses almost exclusively on Equiano the author and the way in which he styles his narrative testimony. Through a narrative subject persona of innocence that learns from the things that happen to him, Equiano forces on his readers a defamiliarization of what they understand as normative. From the narrative subject's perspective, then, the reader comes to see the strange quality of the events that the naive narrator takes as given. Consider the following example, when Equiano reports on his capture:

> The first object that saluted my eyes when I arrived on the coast was the sea, and a slave ship. . . . I was carried on board. I was immediately handled and tossed up to see if I was sound, by some of the crew; and I was now persuaded that I had got into a world of bad spirits, and that they were going to kill me. Their complexions too, differing so much from ours, their long hair,[2] and the language they spoke, which was very different from any I had ever heard, united to confirm me in this belief. Indeed such were the horrors of my views and fears at the moment, that if ten thousand worlds had been my own, I would have freely parted with them all to have exchanged my condition with the meanest slave in my own country. (32–33)

From Equiano's earlier discussion of slavery in his own country and how vastly it differs in character from European slavery, his preference for slavery in Africa here reads all the more poignantly. In this instance, the innocent narrator along with his reader, unlike the experienced author, can be bewildered at the treatment the subject Equiano receives or marvel at the strange customs that appear to be normative among the whites. This establishes a position from which one can make the kind of ironic critique that Equiano perfects in his narrative. My discussion of the *Life* focuses primarily on chapter 5 of the narrative, the climax of the narrative's moral argument.

Modern-day critics have read Equiano's narrative in a variety of different ways and toward a variety of different ends. Keith Sandiford and Angelo Costanzo[3] both read Equiano's narrative primarily as spiritual autobiography. Houston A. Baker equates the slave's emancipation with his mastery of the economics of slavery and claims Equiano's text as the urtext of African American discourse grounded on economic ideology.[4] Joseph Fichtelberg revises Baker's reading by resisting Baker's exclusion of all but the economic model, claiming the need to locate Equiano's narrative in "the context of more comprehensive discursive models."[5] Equiano's narrative clearly functions as a discursive site that engages the variety of debates and discourses that cohere around the question of slavery. That is, the narrative itself elicits such a variety of critical responses because a "good" slave narrative must respond to a number of different academic debates currently waged around the institution of slavery. Fichtelberg makes precisely this point in his critique of Baker's reading of Equiano:

> The problem here involves a conflict between Baker's essentially static model of discursive formation, derived from Foucault, and his activist need for cultural resistance, derived from Marx—of ideology defined both as a construct retrospectively imposed by the critic and as a felt presence against which the writer struggles. (460)

Fichtelberg goes on to suggest that Baker's privileging of the profit motive compels Baker "to deny the force of Equiano's piety, which becomes more, not less, emphatic as the text unfolds" (460).

I do not wish to be misunderstood as devaluing the significance of Baker's critique of Equiano's narrative. On the contrary, Baker's reading opened up entirely new avenues for reading slave narratives that moved us beyond the discussions of history and voice that for a while dominated the study of slave narratives.[6] It showed us that we could risk examining slave literature in more challenging and complicated ways. It showed us that

these narratives participate in discursive practices like those resulting from slave economies. Indeed, it fundamentally introduced discursive concerns into the study of slave narratives.
Some might say that Baker, along with Gates, made possible
much of the even more recent scholarship, influenced by post-
structuralism, that has been written on slave literature. Still,
Baker's reading of Equiano, groundbreaking and compelling as
it is, is really not borne out when one considers the recurring
tropes used by and of concern to abolitionists in the public slavery debates, as attested in the literary and political documents of
the period. Economics was a factor insofar as the greed of the
planter class or the slaveholders was squarely critiqued by white
and black abolitionists, by philosophers such as Montesquieu,
and by political figures such as Thomas Jefferson, whose *Notes on
the State of Virginia*[7] was published in London only two years before Equiano's *Life*. But Baker's claim that Equiano's narrative asserts the narrator's mastery of slave economics as the key to liberation is, I think, overstated.

Consider the following quote from Baker:

The certificate [of manumission] is, in effect, an economic
sign which competes with and radically qualifies the ethical pi-
ousness of its enfolding text. The inscribed document is a
token of mastery, signifying its recipient's successful negotiation of a deplorable system of exchange. The narrator of *The
Life* (as distinguished from the author) is aware of both positive and negative implications of his certificate, and he self-
consciously prevents his audience from bracketing his achievement of manumission as merely an act of virtuous persever-
ance in the face of adversity. "As the form of my manumission
has something peculiar in it, and expresses the absolute power
and dominion one man claims over his fellow, I shall beg leave
to present it before my readers at full length." (36)

Here, for the first time in his argument, we find Baker distinguishing between Equiano the author and Equiano the narrator. Prior to this moment, Baker moves between the two figures with little regard for this distinction. This passage also seems a rather willful misreading of Equiano's purpose in the statement Baker quotes. Before the appearance of this passage in the text, we have been given a full description of the process leading up the manumission. The moment that Baker cites is clearly meant to punctuate the irony of slave possession, which Equiano has been developing until this point in the narrative. It is not meant to undermine the importance of the piety of the narrative, which Baker seems intent on de-emphasizing, but rather to offer further support and evidence to the narrative's critique of the slave system, which is continually represented as absurd, cruel, and immoral (terms familiar to the vernacular of abolitionist rhetoric). Finally, if Equiano was styling his testimony to intervene in the debates around slavery contemporary to himself, he would certainly have been speaking in terms that would have more currency with his contemporary audience than the Marxist paradigm Baker wants to map onto Equiano's narrative.

If Equiano's narrative, as Joseph Fichtelberg suggests, participates in and trades on a complex economy of the image of Africa and of the African that was current in the late eighteenth century, any critical determination of the political ends toward which such economic concerns function in the narrative must include careful attention to the structure of the text itself. I now turn to examine the structure of the narrative in relation to the development of its moral argument against slavery.

The narrative begins in Africa, with the narrator's descriptions of his native customs and people. In these descriptions are many comparisons of his compatriots to the supposedly "more civilized people" of Europe, in which the depictions of his people emerge as morally superior. This portion of the narrative concludes in chapter 2 with Equiano's description of his first encounter with whites, which takes place aboard a slave ship on the coast of Africa. From this moment until chapter 5, Equiano amasses (through his description and subsequent indictment of various incidents of horror and ill treatment of Africans by whites) evidence for his moral disapproval of the behavior of whites. This moral disapproval receives its greatest articulation in chapter 5 of the *Life*, which is devoted almost entirely to a moral condemnation and philosophical refutation of slavery. From chapter 5 through the end of his narrative, Equiano essentially fortifies what we may call—in spite of his expressed designs to the contrary in the opening paragraph of the narrative—his "sainthood" and describes his conversion to Christianity as being in opposition to white "barbarity" and immorality.

My division of the narrative into three phases is not new. Robert Allison and Angelo Costanzo have similarly described the narrative's structure.[8] Each, however, positions Equiano's Christian conversion itself as the climax of the narrative. Still other critics have argued that the conversion is a ruse that Equiano uses—in much the way that Wheatley uses religious rhetoric, as I argued in chapter 4—to identify with his white readership. So much was this the prevailing opinion in 1993 that it prompted critic Katalin Orban to write:

> The current critical consensus, however, questions the seriousness of the conversion and acculturation rhetoric deployed in the narrative. Several contemporary critics, such as Valerie Smith, Chinssole, and Wilfred D. Samuels, see the Christian rhetoric as disguise, Equiano's affirmations of his acculturation as tongue-in-cheek comments, his pride in his achievements as the pride of the African warrior, and, if none of the above are true, his whole narrative as a sad example of mental colonization.[9]

Whether or not the conversion was a serious matter personally for Equiano, I am interested in de-emphasizing the central
role his conversion has enjoyed in the critical response to his
work. I argue instead that when we read the structure of the
narrative as a moral testimony against slavery, the narrative actually climaxes in chapter 5—with the culmination of Equiano's moral argument. Seen in this way, the conversion plays a
supporting role in the last phase of the narrative, the purpose
of which is to legitimate the author as a truly saintly figure, thus
authorizing the force of his moral argument against slavery.
The further development of the author's sainthood, from its la-
borious description of his search for salvation to his desire to
be a missionary, serves both to undergird the legitimacy and
the authority of the moral critique that he has made up to this
point in the narrative and to render his critique of slavery
more palatable to his readers. The reason Equiano gives this
final portion of the narrative so much space, and the reason
that so much of Equiano criticism has focused on the conversion, is that it answers most effectively and explicitly the contemporary Enlightenment arguments that the African is unable to be Christianized.

Robert J. Allison, in his introduction to the 1995 Bedford edition of Equiano's narrative, takes Equiano at his word when
Equiano writes: "I offer here the history of neither a saint, a hero,
nor a tyrant."[10] Allison concludes that "during his [Equiano's]
travels and adventures in this strange world, he is an average
man, as he says 'neither a saint, a hero, nor a tyrant,' but an ordinary person forced to lead an extraordinary life" (2). Comparing Equiano to Ottobah Cugano, Allison insists that Equiano is
but an ordinary man:

Though Cugano had experienced the middle passage and life
in slavery just as Equiano had, his book is a sermon against slav-

ery, not the story of one man's struggle with the institution. Learning from Cugano's experience, Equiano cut down on the sermons, presenting himself instead as an argument against slavery, creating himself as a character with whom ordinary readers would empathize. (19)

Certainly, Cugano's narrative is more spiritually centered than Equiano's, but to claim that Equiano is less pious than Cugano is still to leave a great deal of room for piety on the part of Equiano. Furthermore, Allison does not take seriously enough Equiano's use of an ironic pose in relating his experience. Consider the opening of the narrative itself:

I believe it is difficult for those who publish their own memoirs to escape the imputation of vanity. Nor is this the only disadvantage under which they labour; it is also their misfortune, that whatever is uncommon is rarely, if ever, believed, and from what is obvious we are apt to turn with disgust, and to charge the writer of it with impertinence. People generally think those memoirs only worthy to be read or remembered which abound in great or striking events; those in short, which, in high degree, excite admiration or pity; all others they consign to contempt and oblivion. It is therefore, I confess, not a little hazardous in a private and obscure individual, and a stranger too, thus to solicit the indulgent attention of the public; especially when I own I offer here the history of neither a saint, a hero, nor a tyrant. I believe there are a few events in my life which have not happened to many. It is true that the incidents of it are numerous; and did I consider myself an European, I might say my sufferings were great; but when I compare my lot with that of my countrymen, I regard myself as a *particular favorite of Heaven*, and acknowledge the mercies of Providence in every occurrence of my life. (11–12)

Here, Equiano invokes a well-established stylistic topos of humility in presenting a personal narrative before the public. Still, a great deal of what might initially be observed as humility on the part of Equiano is only a convention. Equiano is keenly aware of the discursive terrain into which this narrative enters. He is entering a discourse in which the very authenticity of slaves' narratives is placed under suspicion. He enters a discourse in which the very humanity of the African is being questioned. Specifically, he enters a discourse in which the question of whether the African can become a Christian is evidence for their humanity. Equiano is keenly aware of how he must make use of the conventions available to him in order to negotiate these various questions. When he states, "People generally think those memoirs only worthy to be read or remembered which abound in great or striking events; those in short, which, in high degree, excite admiration or pity. . . . It is therefore, I confess, not a little hazardous in a private and obscure individual, and a stranger too, thus to solicit the indulgent attention of the public; especially when I own I offer here the history of neither a saint, a hero, nor a tyrant," we are not to take him literally. On the contrary, Equiano often utilizes this humble pose ironically to serve the political purposes of his narrative. His narrative is, in fact, precisely what he says it is not—full of "striking events." When Equiano states that he offers "here the history of neither a saint, a hero, nor a tyrant," he speaks with irony; for in fact, Equiano will assert his moral superiority. His long road to Christian redemption is represented in the text as nothing short of heroic. Even in this "modest" beginning, he asserts that he is "a particular favorite of Heaven."

Let us now examine a few key moments in Equiano's description of his native land and of his compatriots, to see how he positions himself as eyewitness and the ends toward which his testimony is structured.[11] Early in his description of his birthplace, Equiano writes:

This kingdom is divided into many provinces or districts; in one of the most remote and fertile of which, named Essaka, situated in a charming fruitful vale, I was born, in the year 1745. The distance of the province from the capital of Benin and the sea coast must be very considerable; for I had never heard of white men or Europeans, nor of the sea; and our subjection to the king of Benin was little more than nominal. Every transaction of the government, as far as my slender observation extended, was conducted by the chiefs or elders of the place. (12)

Equiano establishes in this passage much of the logical basis for the moral argument against slavery that is to follow. Notice first the idyllic nature of his description of his birthplace. This is further demonstrated later in the narrative, when he describes the vegetation of his country:

Our land is uncommonly rich and fruitful, and produces all kinds of vegetables in great abundance. We have plenty of Indian corn, and vast quantities of cotton and tobacco. Pineapples grow without culture; they are about the size of the largest sugar loaf, and finely flavored. We have also species of different kinds, particularly of pepper; and a variety of delicious fruits which I have never seen in Europe; together with gums of various kinds, and honey in abundance. (17)

The image of Africa with which we are presented is a classically arcadian pastoral landscape, reminiscent of both the biblical Eden and the promised land of Canaan, which flows with milk and honey. It is a land of plenty, with a relaxed, decentralized form of governance. He even suggests that the subjection to the king of Benin was more symbolic than real.

Costanzo points out the extent to which Equiano relied on Anthony Benezet's *Some Historical Account of Guinea* for much of his description in chapter 1 of *Life*. The fact that Equiano used Benezet as a source in this way fortifies my argument, since Benezet himself was, as Costanzo relates, "one of the many Quakers who wrote against slavery in the eighteenth century. His histories of Africa and the slave trade enlightened many whites who had been unaware of the inhumanities of slavery and who had thought of Africa as a dark, crocodile-infested jungle" (55). Costanzo points out how closely Equiano borrows from Benezet by citing two long passages from each text. I reproduce a brief excerpt from each here:

[Benezet]

   That part of Africa from which the Negroes are sold to be carried into slavery, commonly known by the name of Guinea, extends along the coast three to four thousand miles. Beginning at the river Senegal, . . . the land of Guinea takes a turn to the eastward, extending that course about fifteen hundred miles, including those several divisions known by the name of the Grain Coast, and the Slave Coast, with the large kingdom of Benin.

[Equiano]

   That part of Africa known by the name of Guinea, to which the trade for slaves is carried on, extends along the coast above 3400 miles, from Senegal to Angola, and includes a variety of kingdoms. Of these the most considerable is the kingdom of Benin, both as to extent and wealth, the richness and cultivation of the soil, the power of its king, and the number and warlike disposition of the inhabitants. (Costanzo 55)

By choosing Benezet as his model, Equiano gives his work an additional layer of credibility with his white readership. After all, it is the credibility of his testimony that is at stake in the production of Equiano's larger moral argument against slavery that is the *Life*.

Such Edenic representations recur in many of Equiano's descriptions of his native land. Consider the following example:

> All our industry is exerted to improve those blessings of nature. Agriculture is our chief employment; and every one, even to children and women, is engaged in it. Thus we are habituated to labour from our earliest years. Every one contributes something to the common stock: and as we are unacquainted with idleness, we have no beggars. The benefits of such a mode of living are obvious. (17)

The importance of this passage is that it implicitly addresses many of the common stereotypes about Blacks that had currency at the time. For example, though we cannot be certain whether Equiano had read Thomas Jefferson's *Notes on the State of Virginia*, it is clear from the foregoing passage that he was conversant with the discursive milieu from which that text emerged. In many ways, Jefferson's rhetoric of African inferiority in *Notes* well articulates the dominant tropes of African inferiority found more widely distributed among Jefferson's contemporaries. So even if Equiano had not read Jefferson specifically, he would have undoubtedly been familiar with the terms of Jefferson's arguments, which themselves had wide distribution.[12] Thus, many of the terms that Jefferson uses to argue the inferiority of the African in *Notes* are specifically answered by Equiano in *Life*.

In *Notes*, Jefferson favors a system of gradual emancipation, in which Blacks are trained and cared for until a certain age, when they shall be equipped with certain necessary items to be colonized "to such a place as the circumstances of the time should render most proper" (138). To fill the gaps in the society left by these recolonized Africans, Jefferson favors the importation of white settlers from various ports. In anticipation of his reader's possible concern, Jefferson raises the following rhetorical question: "Why not retain and incorporate the blacks into the state, and thus save the expense of supplying, by importation of white settlers, the vacancies they will leave?" To this query, Jefferson's response is most revealing:

> Deep rooted prejudices entertained by whites; ten thousand recollections, by blacks, of the injuries they have sustained; new provocations; the real distinctions which nature has made; and many other circumstances, will divide us into parties, and produce convulsions which will probably never end but in the extermination of the one or the other race.—To these objections, which are political, may be added others, which are physical and moral.[13] (138)

It is these "physical and moral" distinctions to which Equiano so clearly responds. I consider here two of the most prominent claims that Jefferson makes.

The first difference that Jefferson accounts for is that of color. He speculates on what causes the blackness of the African and concludes that whatever the cause, "the difference is fixed in nature" (138). He further argues that skin color is the "foundation of a greater or less share of beauty in the two races," and that the "fine mixtures of red and white, the expressions of every passion by greater or less suffusions of colour in the one, [is] preferable to that eternal monotony, which reigns in . . . that immoveable veil of black which covers all the emotions of the other race" (138). Equiano, while compelled by some of the same climatological theories that held sway with Jefferson on the issue of complexion, argues against Jefferson's view. He contends that race mixing and extended periods of time spent in certain climates have changed the complexion of many, including the Spanish and the Portuguese. He cites how the Spanish who have inhabited the torrid climate of America have become as dark as the Native Americans of Virginia. He punctuates the logic of his argument by adding the statement: "Surely the minds of the Spaniards did not change with their complexions!" (24). It may be worth reiterating that Equiano does not argue against the terms of climatology to defeat the arguments proffered by Jefferson and his contemporaries; rather, he functions within the terms of their argument to render his critique all the more persuasive. This represents one of the hallmarks of Equiano's rhetorical strategy.

The second claim Jefferson makes is that Africans everywhere fail to avail themselves of the "conversation of their masters" (140). By this Jefferson means that Africans have any number of opportunities to learn the art and handicraft of Europeans and to be liberally educated. But they have not the native ability to do so, which Jefferson claims the Native Americans, by contrast, exhibit:

> The Indians, with no advantages of this kind, will often carve figures on their pipes not destitute of design and merit. They will crayon out an animal, a plant, or a country, so as to prove the existence of a germ in their minds which only wants cultivation. They astonish you with strokes of the most sublime oratory; such as prove their reason and sentiments strong, their imagination glowing and elevated. But never yet could I find that a black had uttered a thought above the level of plain narration; never see even an elementary trait of painting or sculpture. (140)

Jefferson continues by denigrating the poetry of Phillis Wheatley and the letters of Ignatius Sancho, even as he casts doubt on the authenticity of both of these as examples of African cultural production.

Equiano responds to such claims first by identifying his compatriots as "almost a nation of dancers, musicians, and poets" (14). This declaration is followed by an elaborate description of the kinds of festivities and public celebrations that occasion the display of these artistic talents. In a footnote, Equiano also tells his reader that while in Smyrna, he "frequently saw the Greeks dance after this manner" (14). This comparison with the Greeks is significant in that it legitimates the cultural practices of the Africans to an audience who would readily acknowledge the superiority of the Greeks' cultural practices. As to the Jeffersonian argument concerning the lack of native ability of the Africans, Equiano's response is equally compelling:

> Are there not causes enough to which the apparent inferiority of an African may be ascribed, without limiting the goodness of God, and supposing He forbore to stamp understanding on what is certainly his own image, because "carved in ebony"? Might it not be naturally ascribed to their situation? When they come among Europeans, they are ignorant of their language, religion, manners, and customs. Are any pains taken to teach them these? Are they treated as men? Does slavery itself depress the mind, and extinguish all its fire, and every noble sentiment? But above all, what advantages do not a refined people possess over those who are rude and uncultivated! Let the polished and haughty European recollect that his ancestors were once like the Africans, uncivilized and barbarous. Did Nature make them inferior to their sons? And should they too have been made slaves? Every rational mind answers, "No." (24)

This is the first in a series of arguments presented by Equiano in the form of rhetorical questions. Equiano here raises a theological objection to the argument for native African inferiority. If God made us all in the image of God, and if God is all powerful and good, we limit God's goodness when we suggest that God would not dispense reason or understanding equally to all. This claim is compelling because it resonates with the late Puritans' claim for a democratic access to salvation, which followed the Great Awakening in America and may have roots as far back as the Half-Way Covenant in the mid–seventeenth century. Equiano contends that any disparity between African and European cultivation is caused by the condition of slavery itself. What Jefferson and others claim as native inferiority Equiano insists is the result of the caste and class divisions within the condition of slavery, divisions that deny the African the opportunity to improve him- or herself. And in those cases where the African does improve him- or herself, as in the case of Equiano and Wheatley, the achievement results either from Herculean efforts or from unusual benevolence shown toward the African. By structuring his argument in terms of rhetorical questions, Equiano skillfully forces the reader, if not to speak aloud, at least to think the answer to the questions he poses. By so doing, he forces a liberationist response, or what he here calls a "rational" response, into the minds of his reading audience. He also rhetorically aligns himself—as author, as the one structuring the argument—with rationality.

Equiano thus refutes the claims of African native inferiority by presenting himself in the narrative as living proof of the African's ability to reason and to master European forms of philosophy and cultural production. This logic not only underlies much of the modern-day criticism of Equiano's *Life* but also goes far to explain the way in which this kind of slave narrative testimony functioned as evidence for the abolitionist movement itself, as I discuss in chapter 1. This display of the narrator's ability to reason is, I argue, what makes chapter 5 of the *Life* central to any understanding of the larger moral critique toward which the narrative moves.

Equiano's narrative frequently reverses the terms of barbarity and savagery, both in serious and in comic ways. Equiano speaks of the "barbarity" to which he is a "witness" (89). Since a witness is always removed temporally and/or spatially from the experience that he or she is witnessing, Equiano is here using the term *barbarity* to describe his Other (Europeans in this case). This rhetorical free play also establishes the force of ironic humor in Equiano's narrative. His deliberate reversal of many of the ethnographic claims of difference or otherness on which Jefferson relies in his *Notes* (and which animate any number of travel narratives from the period) creates moments of authentic humor. For instance, Equiano faints on board the slaveship, after having been "overpowered with horror and anguish" at the first sight of whites and the strangeness of their ways:

> When I recovered a little [from the fainting spell], I found some black people about me . . . they talked in order to cheer me, but all in vain. I asked them if we were not to be eaten by those *white men with horrible looks, red faces, and long hair.* They told me I was not: and one of the crew brought me a small portion of spirituous liquor in a wine glass; but, being afraid of him, I would not take it out of his hand. One of the blacks therefore took it from him and gave it to me, and I took a little down my palate. (33; my emphasis)

Here, Equiano the author forces the reader to see the strangeness of the whites from the perspective of those who are usually understood by the European reader as the Other.

The chief goal of chapter 5 of *Life* is to testify to the details and the character of slave existence. Equiano wants the reader to know the psychological, spiritual, and moral toll that slavery exacts on both the slave and, not insignificantly, the master. When one belongs absolutely to another, one literally lives and exists at the pleasure of one's owner, as Equiano shows. An example of this condition is presented early in chapter 5 of *Life*, when Equiano describes the difference in treatment he received in the transition from the first to the second lady in his "master's good graces" (68). The first lady prized and esteemed Equiano very highly, while to the latter he "was not so great a favourite," since "she had conceived a pique against me, on some occasion when she was on board, and she did not fail to instigate my master to treat me in the manner he did" (68). In a footnote in the text to this moment, Equiano further clarifies that there was a rivalry between the two women:

> Thus was I sacrificed to the envy and resentment of this woman, for knowing that the other lady designed to take me into her service; which, had I got once on shore, she would not have been able to prevent. She felt her pride alarmed at the superiority of her rival in being attended by a black servant: it was not less to prevent this, than to be revenged on me, that she caused the captain to treat me thus cruelly. (68n.)

Another example of such caprice is presented in the anecdote Equiano relates of a "poor Creole Negro" he knew, who would employ himself fishing in his leisure time. Often his master, when he caught any fish, would take them from him without pay. At other times, other whites would do the same. Equiano quotes the slave:

> "Sometimes when a white man take away my fish I go to my master, and he get me my right; and when my master, by strength, take away my fishes, what me must do? I can't go to anybody to be righted; then," said the poor man, looking

up above, "I must look up to God Mighty in the top for right." (79–80)

This story should remind us of an earlier moment in the narrative, when Equiano describes a sailor taking his guinea and falsely promising to get Equiano off the ship that he was desirous to leave. Each of these instances demonstrates the extent to which slaves exist at the whims of their masters and the absence of any "right" to which they may appeal. There is, for the slave, no authority above that of the master, except the ultimate, providential authority of God.

As a result of these conditions, the slave enters, in the logic of Equiano's argument, a mood of utter despair, which eventually spirals downward into a death wish. The clearest example of this descent takes place after Equiano has been purchased by Robert King and is aboard his new master's ship, leaving behind his former master and all that was once valued and familiar to him:

What tumultuous emotions agitated my soul when the convoy got under sail, and I a prisoner on board, now *without hope*! I kept my swimming eyes upon the land in a state of *unutterable grief*; not knowing what to do and *despairing* how to help myself. *While my mind was in this situation*, the fleet sailed on, and in one day's time I lost sight of the wished for land. In the first expression of my grief, I reproached my fate, and wished I had never been born. I was ready to curse the tide that bore us; the gale that wafted my prison, and even the ship that conducted us; and, in the *despair of the moment, I called upon death to relieve me from the horrors I felt and dreaded, that I might be in that place*
　*Where slaves are free and men oppress no more,*
　*Fool that I was inur'd so long to pain,*
　*To trust to hope, or dream of joy again!*
(68; my emphasis)

By using such eloquent prose to narrate such utter despair, Equiano elevates despair itself (or at least its narration) into a form of resistance. The slave's wish for death not only points out the extent of the horrors of slavery but also threatens property. Slave property that either kills itself or renders itself almost worthless because it no longer has the will to live, and is thereby also no longer susceptible to the fear of torture associated with slavery, is not manageable in or good for a slave economy. Equiano counts on his audience's awareness of this logic.

But how does this art of resistance function for the slave narrator? The Greeks of Nietzsche's *The Birth of Tragedy*, according to Will Durant, "overcome the gloom of their disillusionment with the brilliance of their art: out of their own suffering they made the spectacle of the drama and found that 'it is only as an esthetic phenomenon,' as an object of artistic contemplation of reconstruction, 'that existence and the world appear justified.'"[14] If Nietzsche's Greeks overcome the gloom of their disillusionment and pessimism with the brilliance of the Dionysian strain in their art, especially the drama, how does the slave overcome the kind of utter despair witnessed in *Life?*

Before responding to this question, I speak briefly to one difference between the narrative representations in the testimonies of Holocaust survivors, a paradigm for some of my thinking about witnessing to slavery, and those in the testimonies of slaves. Significantly, Holocaust survivors' testimonies often invoke what we may call the "live-to-tell" trope.[15] This trope stands in stark opposition to the repeated recurrence of the death wish in slave testimony. What are we to make of this difference? And more to the point, how does it help us address the larger question concerning the slave's response to utter despair?

These are questions that can be answered properly only when we take into account the issues of location and subject position. It is interesting to note Equiano's representation of his social

location to the "slave" as well. He never appears to take on that
identity for himself. One constantly feels that instead of using the
term as a communal signifier that includes him, "slave" always
signifies something other for Equiano, something outside the essential self he has constructed (a topic to which we will return in
short order). This is, of course, suggestive for the history of black
intellectual production. It parallels in some ways the contemporary problem of social location and representational politics for
modern-day African American intellectuals. That is, the speaking
subject represents and, indeed, trades on the "authentic" experience of those black subjects who do not speak to and/or do not
have access to the rarified and often influential circles in which
black intellectuals speak and circulate.

Significantly, the passage in which Equiano represents his despair and his death wish is uttered by the narrator while aboard a
ship departing from land. The ship, beyond its literal existence,
functions as a spatial metaphor for Equiano. Much of the narrative takes place aboard ships, which transport both the narrator
and the narrative to different locales. What unites these locales,
however, is the condition of slavery. Equiano himself comments
on this situation:

> Nor was such usage as this [he refers here specifically to the
> Creole whose fish were taken from him] confined to particular
> places or individuals; for, in all the different islands in which I
> have been (and I have visited no less than fifteen) the treat-
> ment of the slaves was nearly the same; so nearly, indeed, that
> the history of an island, or even a plantation, with a few such
> exceptions as I have mentioned might serve for a history of the
> whole. (80)

Whereas slavery was widespread—from various sites in Europe
and the East to colonial slavery in the British West Indies, the

French colonies, and the American South—the Holocaust experience was spatially circumscribed. As a historical event with ramifications that we are still just coming to know and understand, the Holocaust was more site specific. I trust this will not be read in any way as an effort to rank oppressions. While I am aware that there are those who have tried to quantify human suffering in this way, and some who continue to do so, let me be clear that I have no interest in such projects. This is, however, an effort to account for the specificity of the circumstances of both of these historical events, in order to determine what creates the difference in the narrative responses to them. Let me suggest, following Shoshana Felman and Dori Laub in *Testimony: Crises of Witnessing in Literature, Psychoanalysis, and History*, not only that the "live-to-tell"[16] trope became a unifying call to action among many in the concentration camps but that it was possible precisely because of the implicit belief on the part of the victim that this thing that was being done to them was temporary, aberrant, and certainly locatable. One could still imagine the possibility of another life beyond the barbed-wire fences of the camps, a world in which this thing was not happening or a time when it would have ceased to happen.

This is unlike what Equiano represents slavery to be. From place to place, everywhere he was taken, the condition of slavery followed him and others like him, extending even to the treatment of "freemen." The condition of slavery became primary to black social identity. Even aboard a ship on the ocean—one of the ultimate Romantic symbols of the vastness, greatness, and unboundedness of nature—Equiano experiences his most powerful despair, his death wish. All of nature seems to collude against him in that pivotal narrative moment: "I was ready to curse the tide that bore us; the gale that wafted my prison, and even the ship that conducted us" (68). The sea itself becomes a metaphorical prison for Equiano in the moment of his despair. Slavery, to the mind of the narrator, converts even the forces of nature to its cause, so that there is no escape from its domain. It is the impossibility of escaping slavery, even imaginatively, that finally leads to despair and the ultimate death wish. Indeed, the Thomas Day poem the narrator quotes represents him as having been a fool "to trust to hope, or dream of joy again" (68). All sense of possibility is emptied out, destroyed.

In this sense, Equiano becomes an impossible witness. He witnesses the impossibility of the situation and the condition of the slave. But, at the same time, his life and his narrative bear witness to the very viability of the impossible witness. That the reader is reading the narrative is a testament to the fact that the narrator does find a way out of his impossible situation, if only through what Cornel West has called, in a different but related context, audacious hope.[17] Let me suggest that for the slave, testimony and an often-related fervent religiosity function like the Dionysian strain in the drama does for Nietzsche's Greeks. That is, the cultural artifacts that most vividly represented the means by which and through which slaves survived and found meaning in their lives were verbal testimony and a belief in a benevolent Christian God.

Equiano's final critique of slavery in chapter 5 of *Life* focuses on slavery's corruption of whites. The argument is steeped, on the one hand, in a deep and abiding Christian morality and, on the other, in Jean-Jacques Rousseau's ideas concerning the origin of inequality among men.[18] Together with Locke's understanding of the mind of man as a *tabula rasa*, these ideas allow Equiano not to blame white men for slavery but rather to condemn what slavery and the avarice that produces it make of man. On these grounds, Equiano finds slavery to be immoral. One portion of his argument emerges when he tells the story of a white man who came aboard the ship *St. Eustatia* to buy some fowl and pigs from him. The man, who Equiano calls a "depredator," returns a day later, demanding the return of his money. Equiano represents this white depredation as common. Equiano refuses to return the money, and the man, seeing that the captain is not aboard, threatens to take the money from him through force. Equiano narrates the conclusion of the story in this way:

> I therefore expected, as my captain was absent, that he would be as good as his word; and he was just proceeding to strike me, when fortunately a British seaman on board, *whose heart had not been debauched by a West-India climate*, interposed and prevented him. But had the cruel man struck me, I certainly should have defended myself, at the hazard of my life. For what is life to a man thus oppressed? (78; my emphasis)

This language of "the heart" not "debauched by a West-India climate" suggests the possibility of the human heart's purity, even the reclaimability of the slave owner's heart. Reminiscent of the racial theories of climatology that had currency in the eighteenth century, Equiano's astute understanding of the impact of the social-political-economic racial "climate" on the "hearts" of whites demonstrates both the generous and redemptive aspects of his humanity and represents white people's natures under slavery as having, to use Rousseau's term, "deteriorated." Ultimately, this kind of circuitous or discursive reasoning about white humanity and slave morality allows Equiano, as he bears witness to the cruelties of slavery for Blacks, also to witness to the deterioration of whites' morality under slavery.

Equiano should not be understood, however, as equating the effects of slavery on blacks with its effects on whites. On this distinction he is remarkably clear. Note his near-justification of retaliatory violence on the part of the slave in the passage above. Equiano may be an early moral precursor for Kingian nonviolent protest, but he is just as much a precursor for Malcom X's radical, revolutionary political struggle.

Consider first Equiano's allusion to the following biblical moment of Jesus speaking in the temple:

> And there was delivered unto him the book of the prophet Esaias. And when he had opened the book, he found the place where it was written, "The Spirit of the Lord is upon me, because he hath anointed me to preach the gospel to the poor; he hath sent me to heal the brokenhearted, to preach deliverance to the captives, and recovering of sight to the blind, to set at liberty them that are bruised, to preach the acceptable year of the Lord." And he closed the book, and he gave it again to the minister, and sat down. And the eyes of the synagogue were fastened on him. And he began to say unto them, "This day is this scripture fulfilled in your ears." (Luke 4:17–21, King James Version)

Equiano relates the frequency of the advantage taken of slaves who, on their own time, "after toiling all day for an unfeeling owner," gather some portions of grass that they bind and take to town to sell (77). He recounts what a common practice it is for white people to take these from the slaves without paying. In addition to this kind of cruel use, he refers to the "constant practice with our clerks, and other whites, to commit violent depredations on the chastity of the female slaves" (74). To this he proclaims:

> Is this one common and crying sin enough to bring down God's judgement on the islands? He tells us the oppressor and the oppressed are both in his hands; and if these are not the poor, the broken-hearted, the blind, the captive, the bruised, of which our Saviour speaks, who are they? (78)

Equiano here equates the misuse of slaves who sell the product of their labors with the sexual abuse of female slaves. The female slaves circulate in a rhetorical moral economy alongside the common, illiterate slave who tells his "artless" tale (notably, the only time Equiano uses dialectal speech in his narrative) that so moves the narrator. Both are characters who deserve pity beyond the shadow of doubt. Rhetorically, then, Equiano trades on the authenticity of their experiences—experiences that he can only witness but that serve to legitimate and authorize the authenticity of his own testimony. In equating them with the wretched and oppressed of whom Jesus speaks,[19] Equiano gestures toward their moral redemption.

Equiano's own response to the man who threatened to take back his money by force serves to help us make the distinction between the moral depravity slavery creates in Blacks as opposed to its manifestation in whites: "But had the cruel man struck me, I certainly should have defended myself, at the hazard of my life. For what is life to a man thus oppressed?" (78). The slave, in other words, commits violent acts because it is the only choice he or she can make in what is otherwise a situation of choicelessness. But Equiano does not forgive the white master's cruelty in the way that he forgives the slave's retaliatory violence:

> Another Negro-man was half hanged, and then burnt, for attempting to poison a cruel overseer. Thus, by repeated cruelties, are the wretched first urged to despair, and then murdered, because they retain so much of human nature about them as to wish to put an end to their misery, and to retaliate on their tyrants! (75)

The slave acts out of his "humanity." The extent to which the slave is still connected with his humanity, even after such cruel efforts by white slave masters to demonstrate the slave's inhumanity, is testimony to his morality. The slave is represented as acting from a position of moral superiority and justification,[20] whereas white slave masters are represented as acting out of mere avarice:

> I have sometimes heard it asserted that a Negro cannot earn his master the first cost; but nothing could be further from the truth . . . for, if it be true, why do the planters and merchants pay such a price for slaves? And, above all, why do those who make this assertion, exclaim the most loudly against the abolition of the slave trade? So much are men blinded and to such inconsistent arguments are they driven by mistaken interest! (73–74)

> Surely this traffic cannot be good, which spreads like a pestilence, and taints what it touches! Which *violates that first natural right of mankind, equality and independency,* and gives one man a dominion over his fellows which God could never intend! For it raises the owner to a state as far above man as it depresses the slave below it; and, with all the presumption of human pride, sets distinction between them, immeasurable in extent, and endless in duration! *Yet how mistaken is the avarice even of the planters.* Are slaves more useful by being thus humbled to the condition of brutes, than they would be if suffered to enjoy the privileges of men? The freedom which diffuses health and prosperity throughout Britain answers— "No." (80; my emphasis)

The conclusion of chapter 5 of Equiano's *Life* culminates with what can only be described as a homiletic on the contradictions of the logic that undergirds slave morality. Equiano's reasoning is here grounded in Rousseau's understanding of the origin of inequality among men, and it challenges both the morality and the rationality of slavery. Equiano also takes on (knowingly or unknowingly) Jefferson's position on Africans in his *Notes*. The tone is sober but illustrative of the rage to which Equiano in the end lays claim by invoking the specter of "insurrection":

> *When you make men slaves*, you deprive them of virtue, you set them, in your own conduct, an example of fraud, rapine, and cruelty, and compel them to live with you in a state of war; and yet you complain that they are not honest and faithful! You stupify them with stripes and think it necessary to keep them in a state of ignorance; and yet you assert that they are incapable of learning; that their minds are such a barren soil or moor that culture would be lost on them; and that they come from a climate, where nature, though prodigal in her bounties in a degree unknown to yourselves, has left man alone scant and unfinished, and incapable of enjoying the treasures she has poured out for him!—An assertion at once *impious and absurd.* Why do you use those instruments of torture? Are they fit to be applied by *one rational being to another*? And are ye not struck with shame and mortification, to see *the partakers of your nature* reduced so low? But, above all, are there no dangers attending this mode of treatment? Are you not hourly in dread of an insurrection? (80–81; my emphasis)

The threat of insurrection at the close of chapter 5 of *Life* is interesting especially for the way in which it is made. In the chapter, Equiano invokes John Milton's *Paradise Lost.* This act in itself serves to show that he is a learned man and has read not only the Bible but texts as wide-ranging as Benezet, Milton, and Clarkson. The use of footnotes in the narrative stands as evidence of his erudition. But, specifically, here he cites a passage from *Paradise Lost* spoken by Milton's Satan, who complains of his enslavement to God. The question arises: Why would Equiano align the slave's cause with the cause of Satan against God? Let me suggest that

what we have here is a misreading or misappropriation by Equiano of *Paradise Lost*. Hence, the example should be read as a
canonical literary representation of the resistance to hierarchy
and not as a perfect analogy. Otherwise, we would also have to
equate Satan's cryptic and circuitous logic with Equiano's own
logic. Of course, another possibility is that the example from *Paradise Lost* serves to demonstrate the kind of histrionic arguments
necessitated by the oppressed in situations of intense hierarchy.
In this sense, the analogy is not to the morality of Milton's Satan
but rather to his discursive circumstances of having to create reason from a situation that is thoroughly unreasonable. In the context of Equiano's justification of insurrection, this argument has
some force.

The language of this passage is extremely revealing. First, consider the use of the pronoun *you*. Who is this "you" being addressed directly by the narrator? An answer to this query carries
us far toward an analysis of Equiano's social location in this narrative, or what we might call his identity politics. That is, once we
know to whom this moment in the narrative is addressed, we can
better understand the rhetorical ways in which he is negotiating
his own social location in relation to the slave community (which,
as I briefly discussed earlier, he is never quite comfortably a part
of in any rhetorical sense), as well as the confluence of various
discursive formations. A cursory reading might suggest that the
"you" addressed here are whites generally. But when we consider
the rhetorical actions and thoughts ascribed to this ambiguous
pronoun, the antecedent begins to come into clearer focus. The
"you" of whom Equiano speaks are specifically those posing the
pro-slavery arguments that he so readily and intensely resists.

Equiano also makes clear that he is tutored in, and is here participating in, the discourse of natural rights elaborated by Rousseau (among others), a discourse frequently employed by abolitionists in their anti-slavery arguments. The passage quoted

begins with "When you make men slaves . . ." This assumes, first, that Africans, like Europeans, are indeed "men." They are not a lower species but rather are on a par with the humanity given to all of God's creation under the sign of "man." This is not an insignificant point for an Enlightenment figure, himself a former African slave, to make. And it certainly resonates with the thoughts of Rousseau (in "Discourse on the Origin and Basis of Inequality") on the matter, who believed that

> men are naturally as equal among themselves as were the animals of each species before physical causes had brought about the variations that we now observe in some of them, for it is inconceivable that those first changes, however they may have occurred, should have altered the individual of the species all at once and in the same way. While some improved or deteriorated and acquired various qualities, good or bad, others continued to remain in their original state. (138)

Equiano here uses the language of "one rational being to another" and "partakers in your nature"[21] to further advance the argument of equality among men, in order to point out the immorality of the institution of African slavery. Again he relies on the philosophical discourse of natural rights and an appeal to Enlightenment discourse on "rationality" or "reason." But he also identifies here the grounds on which his main objections to the arguments for slavery rest. He states that the assertions of the pro-slavery advocacy are "at once impious and absurd." These two words, *impious* and *absurd*, identify his critique of slavery and slave morality as both a moral critique (which renders the institution impious) and a philosophical one (which renders it absurd). To Equiano's mind, slavery cannot be convincingly justified through either critique. It is possible, of course, to read this narrative as primarily concerned with the spiritual salvation of the narrator. To do so exclusively, however, would be to ignore the import of the author's Africanness and his participation in the anti-slavery cause. I think, instead, that the narrative is best read as primarily a slave narrative, the purpose of which is to participate in the anti-slavery movement. One of the ways in which it does so is by demonstrating the Christian morality of the narrator, thus arguing for his humanity and the immorality of slavery. Perhaps the most compelling evidence for the narrative being read in this way is that its full title is *The Interesting Narrative of the Life of Olaudah Equiano, or Gustavus Vassa, the African*—not *the Christian—Written by Himself.*

# 6. Consider the Audience

## Witnessing to the Discursive Reader in Douglass's *Narrative*

It takes two to speak the truth—one to speak and another to hear.      —Henry David Thoreau

This chapter brings together some of the concerns discussed in the preceding ones by recasting, in terms that are most familiar to my readers, the discursive terrain into which the slave narrator enters to give his or her testimony. That is, I consider who is the intended reader of the slave's testimony. The search for this reader leads us not to a particular person or even to a particular community of persons. Rather, this discursive reader, which the slave implies in his or her testimony, is in fact a confluence of political, moral, and social discursive concerns that animate, necessitate, and indeed make possible slave testimony itself. In this way, our discursive reader is not altogether unrelated to Benedict Anderson's "imagined communities."[1] The discursive reader, for the slave witness, is the imagined horizon wherein the pro-slavery advocates (and their arguments for slavery), the abolitionists (from the sentimental moralists to the staunchly political Garrisonians), and the ongoing debates between these two over slavery (which are characterized by such discursive sites as black humanity, natural rights, the Christian morality of slavery, the treatment of slaves under slavery, etc.) come together as an entity that will be the recipient of the slave's testimony. Or, put another way, it is this discursive reader who serves as principal witness to the slave witness.

By foregrounding the implied profile of the discursive reader in our reading of Frederick Douglass's *Narrative of the Life of Frederick Douglass, An American Slave: Written by Himself* (1845), we call attention to the various rhetorical strategies employed by slave witnesses in telling their "truth" about slavery. I cite Mikhail Bakhtin here in order to sketch a more thorough understanding of how the profiling of the discursive reader might function as a reading practice for testimonial texts:

> Active understanding . . . , by bringing what is being understood within the new horizon of the understander, establishes a number of complex interrelations, consonances and dissonances with what is being understood, enriches it with new moments. It is precisely this kind of understanding that the speaker takes account of. Therefore his orientation towards the listener is an orientation towards the particular horizon, the particular world of the listener, it introduces completely new moments into his discourse: what takes place here is an interaction of different contexts, different points of view, different horizons, different expressively accented systems, different social "languages." The speaker seeks to orient his discourse with its own determining horizon within the alien horizon of the understander and enters into dialogic relations with moments of that horizon. The speaker penetrates the alien horizon of the listener, constructs his utterance on alien territory, against his, the listener's, apperceptive background. (Quoted in Shepherd, 92)

If we substitute Bakhtin's "speaker" with our "witness," and his "understander" with our "discursive reader," his utility to our situation comes into focus. The slave witness witnesses not only to individuals but also to the "world of the listener," his or her discursive milieu. While Bakhtin sees the listener's world as an "alien horizon," I want to press this point and picture it rather as a mixed or hybrid horizon. This is based in the logic that whites' understanding of slavery functions as public understanding of slavery. Slave experience of slavery, though of great interest to the public, is still "other" to that dominant horizon. That is to say only what racialist logic dictates: Blacks must, for the sake of survival in a racialized context in which they are the oppressed, know whites and their cultural and social logics, while whites are not obliged in the same way to know Blacks. The more aptly the witness accomplishes this speaking to the horizon of the white reader, the more politically effective his or her testimony will be to the cause of abolitionism in this case.

I turn here to the most well known and most often discussed of slave narratives, for reasons having to do with its very celebrity. Douglass's *Narrative* received a great deal of attention nationally and internationally in its day. Much of this had to do, as scholars have more than demonstrated, with its narrative force and rhetorical sophistication. It must also be said that much of its fame had to do with its timing. In the years after the publication of Douglass's *Narrative*, as the nation moved closer to civil war and the number of slave narratives vying for the public's attention grew, it became more difficult for slave narratives to be published. Not unlike American blockbuster films today, with their computerized special effects, the bar is raised each time something new and more exciting comes out. For example, George Lucas's *Star Wars* (20th Century Fox, 1977) was, for its time, an incredible film and retains an important place in American film history for the technical advancements it brought to the medium. Were it released for the first time in the year 2000, however, it would have been a tough sell to a contemporary audience. Similarly, we must remember that among the various other purposes they served, slave narratives were sensational for their time:

Except for Harriet Beecher Stowe's enormously successful *Uncle Tom's Cabin* (1852), the Romantic age in America had no more popular exemplars than the narratives of fugitive slaves. Indeed, the slave autobiographies published in the 1830's and 1840's may have helped prepare the audience for Stowe's classic best-seller. The great antebellum works of Ralph Waldo Emerson, Henry David Thoreau, Walt Whitman, Herman Melville, or Margaret Fuller did not sell nearly as well as the approximately one hundred book-length slave narratives. The epic character of individuals who first *willed* their own freedom, then *wrote* the story proved irresistible to readers in the American North and Britain. Those who would never literally see slavery could find a literary medium through which to observe and perhaps understand it.[2]

So much is this the case that Saidya Hartman, in her illuminating study *Scenes of Subjection: Terror, Slavery, and Self-Making in Nineteenth-Century America,* makes this the point that launches her project. She writes, "At issue here is the precariousness of empathy and the uncertain line between witness and spectator" (4). The sensationalism of slave narratives should not be ignored. That public demands placed on slave testimony included that they be increasingly revealing and even pruriently detailed about suffering under slavery might explain why Harriet Jacobs, for instance, had far more difficulty by 1860—some fifteen years after Douglass's *Narrative* came out—trying to secure publication of her narrative. Still, it makes sense to seek our profile of the discursive reader in this most successful narrative of the nineteenth century. Douglass was clearly aware of his discursive milieu and paid a great deal of attention to this awareness in the crafting of his testimony.

To begin my discussion of Douglass, I turn in the *Narrative* to the clearest statement of both his keen and conscious knowledge of the power he wields as witness and his awareness his readers' desires:

> I deeply regret the necessity that impels me to suppress any thing of importance connected with my experience of slavery. It would afford me great pleasure indeed, as well as materially add to the interest of my narrative, were I at liberty to gratify a curiosity, which I know exists in the minds of many, by an accurate statement of all the facts pertaining to my most fortunate escape. But I must deprive myself of this pleasure, and the curious of the gratification which such a statement would afford. I would allow myself to suffer under the greatest imputations which evil-minded men might suggest, rather than exculpate myself, and thereby run the hazard of closing the slightest avenue by which a brother slave might clear himself of the chains and fetters of slavery. (94)

In this passage, Douglass offers an explanation for the absence of detail in his description of his escape. That he calls attention to this absence suggests that he presumes his readers appreciate that up to this point he has been providing them with great detail. This mention by Douglass further recognizes the implicit relationship, which he himself appreciates in narrative testimony, between "detail" and "desire." Still, for our purposes, this passage accomplishes far more than this; it is also the statement in the *Narrative* wherein Douglass reveals that he is working with a complex understanding of the function and purpose of his testimony. That he deeply regrets that "necessity" impels him to "suppress anything of importance connected with [his] experience in slavery" reiterates to his reader his efforts to disclose fully his slave experience. This further attests to his desire to tell all. He goes even further when he introduces the word *pleasure* in the very next sentence. Douglass's admission that to tell all would afford him "great pleasure" and "add materially" to the interest of his narrative can only be read as a desire to witness. Douglass wants to give his testimony. He even appreciates the pleasure involved in being the one who can bear witness. Herein is the one place where slave experience is a benefit—the role of the eyewitness. Douglass and other slave narrators seem to say that, in the context of the discursive milieu of the African slave, to tell all, to authenticate through no suppression of experience, and to take delight in so doing is what the best and most reliable slave witness does, or at least represents him- or herself as doing.[3] Also in the passage above, Douglass speaks of how full disclosure would "materially add" to the interest of his narrative. Such a statement demonstrates a strong understanding of his readership and of market forces involved in the production of a slave narrative. It also suggests Douglass's desire to pay attention to such forces in his testimony.

The other side of his pleasure in full disclosure is identified by Douglass as the gratification of his reader's "curiosity." This should remind us of Prince's use of her experience and its fetishistic value, discussed in chapter 3. It also points once again to the important implications, addressed by Hartman, regarding the fine line between witness and spectator to which the reader of such narrative cataloging of brutality is subject. Douglass recognizes that there is some of both in his discursive reader and seeks to use such knowledge to his narrative advantage. Still, it should not escape us that the one time in the narrative when Douglass chooses explicitly to deny both his narrative pleasure and the gratification of his reader's curiosity is in the name of "brotherhood" with his fellow slaves. All pleasure and all gratification are subordinated to Douglass's strong belief that he and others must never do anything to limit the chance of other slaves to liberate themselves from "the chains and fetters of slavery." Douglass's self-awareness of purpose here is a fitting start for the examination of the *Narrative* that follows.

Historian David W. Blight, in his introduction to the 1993 Bedford edition of Douglass's *Narrative*, discusses abolitionist newspaper editor Nathaniel P. Rogers's description of Douglass's speech delivered in Concord, New Hampshire, February 11, 1844, saying that the speech

> offers a striking picture not only of Douglass "narrating his early life" but also of an angry young man who insists that Americans imagine slavery as a scene of horror. Rogers's description of the rhetorical pivot in the speech is stunning: Douglass finished narrating the story and "gradually let out the outraged humanity that was laboring within him, in an indignant and terrible speech. It was not what you could describe as oratory or eloquence. It was sterner—darker—deeper than these. It was the volcanic outbreak of human nature long pent up in slavery and at last bursting its imprisonment." (5)

Rogers's description of Douglass helps us see how the abolitionist viewed and prized eyewitness slave testimony as the best evidence against slavery. Again, with all that the abolitionists could do, their rhetoric was not the same as what—to their minds—the slave's testimony brought to the public discursive war over slavery, a fact of which Douglass was well aware.

Blight insists that Douglass's narrative "belonged to the world of abolitionism and to the national political crisis over slavery from which it sprang" (3). I agree with this assessment but would go further to say that it was also a response to the same. It is important to remind ourselves that while white abolitionism and the national debate over slavery did indeed produce the slave witnesses that have come down to us through history, these same witnesses were also acutely aware of the unique value of what they brought to this discourse—their personal experiences of being slaves. So, while much of their testimony was overdetermined by the circumstances of its production (which Blight rightly points out), much of it was also about presenting its unique perspective before the public of abolitionists and pro-slavery advocates alike. After all, if slave testimony had no value in the contemporary debates on slavery over and above what white abolitionists' own reports on slavery had to offer, I dare say that not only would the course and history of African American literary production be markedly different but the cooperation between white and black abolitionists would have been greatly diminished.

Blight maintains that "what sets Douglass apart in the genre [of slave narratives], though, is that he interrogated the moral conscience of his readers, at the same time that he transplanted them into his story, as few other fugitive slave writers did" (8). Whether or not we agree with Blight about Douglass's singularity in this regard (for there is much to suggest that Equiano, for example, did the same, and earlier), that Douglass knew his reader is undeniable. It is this fact that most interests me in my reading of the *Narrative*.

One of the most striking aspects of Douglass's *Narrative* is the self-consciousness with which he understands, profiles, and addresses his discursive reader. Evidence of this is presented throughout the *Narrative*, with its attention to the various tenets of abolitionist discourse (abolitionist needs and concerns for these testimonies, pro-slavery arguments about authenticity and the misrepresentation of Southern slavery, natural rights discourse, religious and moral discourse that tends toward moral suasion, etc.). By focusing our attention on how the discursive reader is constructed implicitly in this text, we begin perhaps to gain the clearest picture yet of the complex discursive terrain that is abolitionist discourse and the numerous demands it placed on the rhetorical strategies used in slave testimony. And if Blight is correct in his view that "slave narratives are, of course, personal testimonies; but they are also the individual stories by which we begin to discern patterns of a collective experience that

we can comprehend as *history*," then taking account of the discursive milieu in which such history comes to be is of the utmost
importance (15).

There are three projects that chapter 1 of the *Narrative* has for
Douglass in relation to his discursive reader. First, it chronicles
the move from childhood innocence into a consciousness of
slave experience. Second, in so doing, it demonstrates the status
of slave epistemology—what slaves know and do not know—so
much so that the words *know* and *knowledge* appear no fewer than
twelve times in this short chapter alone. Third, this chapter is
arranged in two distinct halves with regard to the question of
slave epistemology. The first half, consisting of the first five para-
graphs, is the section in which Douglass constantly equivocates—
purposefully moving back and forth between what he knows and
what he does not know. This shifting back and forth establishes
with the distrustful segment of the collective discursive reader
Douglass's desire for complete veracity. It shows him to be a reliable witness. After all, any witness who would tell you from the
very beginning what he knows as well as what he does not know—
and who even goes to the pains of informing his reader of what
he knows by inference versus what he knows as a matter of fact—
is at the very least concerned, in a decidedly self-conscious way,
with having his reader trust his veracity. The remaining half of
the chapter ceases with equivocation altogether and begins to
make full declarative statements about what the narrator has experienced, almost completely dispensing with the need to speak
about what he does not know. In fact, few negative epistemological statements are made at all in this second half of the chapter.
Having established himself as reliable (and what reader cannot
but be moved by the childhood memories and sympathies Douglass plays on in this chapter?), he is now free to state his case.

The chapter closes with the representation of the loss of childhood innocence about slavery. This loss of innocence is caused

by the beating of his Aunt Hester, which Saidya Hartman labels a
"primal scene" for Douglass:

> I remember the first time I ever witnessed this horrible exhi-
> bition. I was quite a child, but I well remember it. I never
> shall forget it whilst I remember any thing. It was the first of
> a long series of such outrages, of which I was doomed to be a
> witness and a participant. It struck me with awful force. It was
> the blood-stained gate, the entrance to the hell of slavery,
> through which I was about to pass. It was a most terrible spec-
> tacle. I wish I could commit to paper the feelings with which
> I beheld it. (42)

> I was so terrified and horror-stricken at the sight, that I hid
> myself in a closet, and dared not venture out till long after
> the bloody transaction was over. I expected it would be my
> turn next. It was all new to me. I had never seen anything
> like it before. I had always lived with my grandmother on the
> outskirts of the plantation, where she was out to raise the
> children of the younger women. I had therefore been, until
> now, out of the way of the bloody scenes that often occurred
> on the plantation. (43)

Many of the various aspects represented by the discursive reader
cohere in these important passages. The horror of slave corporal
punishment[4] and its spectacularization shame the pro-slavery
reader with the psychological uses to which such public punishments are put by slave owners; at the same time, the episode
speaks to the sympathies of Northern readers who may not be familiar with the brutalities of slavery. For the benefit of the more
sentimental aspect of the discursive reader, much influenced by
Romantic ideology and the loss of innocence, the narrative asso-
ciates this kind of violence with the loss of innocence for the
child Douglass, who witnesses it. It also plays on the fetishistic de-

sire of the spectatorial reader (discussed in chapter 3) to know slavery when Douglass essentially represents his feelings as unrepresentable: "I wish I could commit to paper the feelings with which I beheld it." The geography of the plantation, which Douglass describes at the very end of the *Narrative*'s first chapter, should also remind us of the geographical concerns of abolitionist discourse, referred to earlier in chapter 2. That is, Douglass's position "on the outskirts of the plantation" is not unlike that of Northerners who had limited experience with the actual institution of slavery. In this way, the Northern reader is identified in this rhetorical economy with the innocent child Douglass and, through Douglass's testimony, may also have a primal scene of a sort that might lead to another kind of conversion, from spectator to abolitionist. There is much in this opening chapter of Douglass's *Narrative* to suggest that the witness is well aware of the various aspects of the discursive reader to whom he is addressing his testimony.

In chapter 2 of the *Narrative*, Douglass provides his reader with a description of the first plantation he lived on and of slave life on the plantation. The narrative arc of the chapter moves from description of the landscape and of the mode of production and management of Colonel Lloyd's large plantation system to some intimate details about the domestic lives of the slaves. Douglass demonstrates what Prince makes a point of arguing for in her narrative—that he knows what the slave knows—in statements such as "His death [the overseer Mr. Severe's] was regarded by the slave as the result of a merciful providence." Another example occurs when he reports to the reader what a privilege the slaves thought it was to be asked to run an errand to the "Great House Farm":

> The home plantation of Colonel Lloyd wore the appearance
> of a country village. . . . The whole place wore a business-like
> aspect very unlike the neighboring farms. . . . It was called by

the slaves the *Great House Farm*. Few privileges were esteemed higher, by the slaves of the out-farms, than that of being selected to do errands at the Great House Farm. It was associated in their minds with greatness. . . . He was called the smartest and most trusty fellow, who had this honor conferred upon him the most frequently. The competitors for this office sought as diligently to please their overseers, as the office-seekers in the political parties seek to please and deceive the people. The same traits of character might be seen in Colonel Lloyd's slaves, as are seen in the slaves of the political parties. (45–46)

Scholars have commented on the fact that Douglass may be influenced in this characterization of political parties by the Garrisonian doctrine of anti-partyism, and that "this ironic play on representative democracy also shows Douglass's sense of the slaves' abilities to make the most of their daily lives and of the political and moral economy of slavery" (Blight, 111n. 13). For our purposes, it also shows the extent to which Douglass demonstrates to his discursive reader that he trades on insider information. He knows what the slaves think and how the slaves refer to things. This speaks to the abolitionist need for slave testimony to give eyewitness accounts that reveal information to which white abolitionists do not have direct access. What is also striking in the characterization of political parties in this passage is the metaphorical use of slavery. By the 1840s there was a well-established rhetorical tradition of enlisting the terms *slave* and *slavery* in a variety of other contexts: Wollstonecraft used it to describe the condition of women; Edgeworth used to describe the condition of the Irish; American revolutionaries used it to hyperbolize their relationship to the English; and so on. Douglass would have been well aware of the variety of uses to which *slave* as metaphor could be put. His choice here to make use of that metaphor is rhetorically pointed as well, for it represents the slave, as Blight tells us, as manipulating the moral economy of slavery even as it represents politicians as manipulating the people. Douglass presents neither of these as positive attributes, but he points out both as responses to similarly corrupt institutions—a point Garrisonian abolitionist readers would have gladly received.

Douglass closes chapter 2 with his discussion of the meaning of slave songs. His examination of these would have read most readily to abolitionists of the more sentimental moralist variety:

> I have sometimes thought that the mere hearing of those songs would do more to impress some minds with the horrible character of slavery, than the reading of whole volumes of philosophy on the subject could do.
>
> I did not, when a slave, understand the deep meaning of those rude and apparently incoherent songs. I was myself within the circle; so that I neither saw nor heard as those without might see and hear. They told a tale of woe which was then altogether beyond my feeble comprehension; they were tones loud, long, and deep; they breathed the prayer and complaint of souls boiling over with the bitterest anguish. Every tone was a testimony against slavery, and a prayer to God for deliverance from chains. (47)

Douglass suggests here that there are two interpretive epistemologies with regard to slavery, both equally valuable: there is the knowledge produced and understood in the slave community, and there is the knowledge produced and understood from outside the slave community. Both play a role here, and Douglass, as narrator/slave witness and as the subject of narration, gets to play both roles. It is not until later that he comes to comprehend the "deep meaning" of the slave songs, which he reads as "a testimony against slavery, and a prayer to God for deliverance from chains." This explains why Douglass, as Equiano often did in his narrative, moves from talking about himself in the first person in the opening chapter of his narrative to the voice that vacillates between Douglass as slave witness (the Douglass who writes the narrative) and Douglass the slave (the subject of narration), who offers his descriptions of his own thoughts and feelings as well as those of "slaves" more generally.

"Slave" is a category that Douglass the narrator seems to want to claim firsthand knowledge of but does not want always to claim for himself. This speaks to the tension of presenting oneself to a discursive reader as both the authentic eyewitness to slavery—the former slave (legally, in his case, still a fugitive slave) still connected enough to that community to represent it—and as the cultivated man of letters who produces the narrative and advances the argument for black humanity. This textual tension, not unlike the tension modern-day black "public" intellectuals experience, seems aptly represented here.[5] It is finally the latter Douglass, who can now interpret the slave's songs, who makes the following statement at the end of chapter 2 of the *Narrative*:

> I have often been utterly astonished, since I came to the north, to find persons who could speak of the singing, among slaves, as evidence of their greater contentment and happiness. It is impossible to conceive of a greater mistake. Slaves sing most when they are most unhappy. . . . The singing of a man cast away upon a desolate island might be as appropriately considered as evidence of contentment and happiness, as the singing of a slave; the songs of the one and of the other are prompted by the sane emotion. (47)

In this moment, Douglass speaks to correct erroneous readings of slave singing as evidence of slaves' contentment—very likely stories Northerners picked up from pro-slavery advocates. Addressed explicitly to correct this opinion held by people of the

North, the passage also implicitly speaks to the pro-slavery advocacy and educates Northern readers about how common it is for slavery to be misrepresented for nefarious purposes. This further necessitates and points up the importance of the kind of slave testimony that Douglass himself provides.

The example of the colonel's prized garden, which was the source of so much temptation for the hungry slaves, is an interesting one with which to open chapter 3 of the *Narrative*. It attests to the lunacy and arbitrary nature of slave punishment, and the text does not want for other examples like it. These types of stories, wherein Douglass describes the details of a certain arbitrary situation, such as the colonel tarring the fence around the garden so that any slave caught with tar on him would automatically be punished under suspicion that he had been in the colonel's garden, certainly authenticate the narrative by virtue of reporting with such detail. But in addition to authenticating the narrative, such details present a picture of slavery largely unavailable to the distant Northern reader—proximity to slavery being one of the aspects that concerns the discursive reader. Douglass reports the following:

> Slaves, when inquired of as to their condition and the character of their masters, almost universally say they are contented, and that their masters are kind. The slave holders have been known to send in spies among their slaves, to ascertain their views and feelings in regard to their condition. The frequency of this has had the effect to establish among the slaves the maxim, that a still tongue makes a wise head. They suppress the truth rather than take the consequences of telling it, and in so doing prove themselves a part of the human family. (50)

This, along with the story preceding it of the unfortunate, unwitting slave who answers truthfully when Colonel Lloyd interrogates him, and who is sold away for so doing, seems a direct reply to pro-slavery advocates' rhetoric that slaves are actually quite happy and well taken care of—another aspect of the discursive reader to which Douglass addresses himself. Douglass here is also very astute about what constitutes "truth" and what its shifting parameters are for the slave. Citing the fact that slaves know when to suppress the truth, rather than to "take the consequences of telling it," as testimony to their humanity is striking. Knowing full well how important veracity is to his testimony as slave witness, Douglass discusses the circumstances under slavery that force slaves to lie. By lying, he reasons, they demonstrate their intellect and the use of it as a means of self-preservation. In this way, he concludes, they "prove themselves a part of the human family." Logic so sound and at the same time so circuitous as this can only be the result of Douglass's awareness of a complex discursive reader and the variety of competing demands such complexity places on slave testimony.

As further testament to this awareness, we can turn to Douglass's description of the better treatment of slaves in Baltimore than of those in more rural settings. So impressed is he with Baltimore that he speaks of Providence bringing him to that city:

> I may be deemed superstitious, and even egotistical, in regarding this event as a special interposition of divine Providence in my favor. But I should be false to the earliest sentiments of my soul, if I suppressed the opinion. I prefer to be true to myself, even at the hazard of incurring the ridicule of others, rather than to be false, and incur my own abhorrence. (56)

His willingness, again, to be honest to himself and to speak to the variations in slave treatment (a gesture precisely the opposite of what Equiano made with regard to slavery some fifty years earlier) is a testament to his veracity. It is a direct response to pro-slavery forces' arguments that these narratives were the products of abolitionists trying to represent slavery in a bad light and to make slave owners feel guilty. Even so, Douglass's decision is to end chapter 5 of the *Narrative* (after making this statement about Baltimore) with an example of an exception to this kind of good treatment, in the case of Mary and Henrietta (58–59). Also, at the beginning of this chapter and in the beginning of the next, his description of his mistress and how slavery changed even her kindness by warping it with a sense of the absolute control over another, which slavery instantiates, gives the sense of slavery as an institution that forces identities on both slave and master. Both have to learn to play their parts in the drama that is slavery. The opposite effects on Douglass and his mistress of Mr. Auld's speech against teaching Douglass to read, for example, is very telling in this regard. For the former, Mr. Auld's opposition made him more resolved than ever to learn to read and taught him that a great part of the power of the master over the slave was in keeping the slave ignorant of his lot. The mistress, however, became bitterly opposed to any efforts on Douglass's part to learn to read and began to treat him more harshly. Still, both parties recognized the partial origin of slavery's power over slaves—keeping slaves ignorant through illiteracy.

Another aspect of abolitionism that garners Douglass's full attention in his narrative is the rhetorical use of religion by the institution of slavery. Especially in chapter 9 of the *Narrative*, Douglass is concerned to point out the irony of religion's effects on the hearts of slaveholders. One such example of his heavy critique can be seen in this passage:

> I have said Master Thomas was a mean man. He was so. Not to give a slave enough to eat, is regarded as the most aggravated development of meanness even among slave holders. The rule is, no matter how coarse the food, only let there be enough of it. . . . Master Thomas gave us enough of neither coarse nor

fine food. . . . We were therefore reduced to the wretched necessity of living at the expense of our neighbors. This we did by
begging and stealing, whichever came handy in the time of
need, the one being considered as legitimate as the other. A
great many times have we poor creatures been nearly perishing
with hunger, when food in abundance lay mouldering in the
safe and smoke-house, and our pious mistress was aware of the
fact; and yet that mistress and her husband would kneel every
morning, and pray that God would bless them in basket and
store! (68)

Remarkable for how it relates the neglect of a basic human need
for food—with which any reader can identify—to the supposed
Christian piety of the master and mistress, this passage is em-
blematic of Douglass's critique of slaveholder religion. Douglass
also makes clear to the reader that such hypocritical treatment by
slaves of Christians has the effect of reducing the slave to a state
of moral depravity, resulting in "begging and stealing." In this
way, he not only elicits sympathy for the moral choices to which
such neglect leads the slave but leaves open the possibility of
other kinds of moral depravity of which slavery may make the
slave capable. This would play into the logic of those abolitionist
readers whose concerns over slavery originated from a concern
with what slavery did to the possibility for the moral education of
the slave, and therefore to the possibility of the slave's salvation.

    That there be no doubt as to his critique of religion, Douglass
also directly relates religion to corporal violence against slaves. In
a passage that follows a nearly two-page-long discussion of what a
"mean" man his master was, Douglass offers up the following observation of religion's relationship to violence against slaves:

    I have said my master found religious sanction for his cruelty.
    As an example, I will state one of many facts going to prove the

charge. I have seen him tie up a lame young woman, and whip her with a heavy cowskin upon her naked shoulders, causing the warm red blood to drip; and, in justification of the bloody deed, he would quote this passage of Scripture—"He that knoweth his master's will, and doeth it not, shall be beaten with many stripes." (70)

In addition to demonstrating the dangers of a system in which people exercise absolute control over the lives of others, this passage shows how such exercise of power justified itself and its violence by means of the very religion that many abolitionists believed condemned slavery. This is also an attack on that aspect of Douglass's discursive reader which believed that slaves were not equal to whites and were therefore better off in slavery, where at least they were "taken care of." My reading of Maria Edgeworth in chapter 2 might be recalled as representative of this aspect of the discursive reader. Douglass's ironic reply to such claims is simply that "Master Thomas was one of the many pious slave holders who hold slaves for the very charitable purpose of taking care of them" (70).

He returns to this theme in chapter 10, when he makes the following damning statement about religion:

I assert most unhesitatingly, that the religion of the south is a mere covering for the most horrid crimes,—justifier of the most appalling barbarity,—and sanctifier of the most hateful frauds,—and dark shelter under which the darkest, foulest, grossest, and most infernal deeds of slave holders find the strongest protection. Were I to be again reduced to the chains of slavery, next to that enslavement, I should regard being the slave of a religious master the greatest calamity that could befall me. For of all the slave holders with whom I have ever met, religious slave holders are the worst. I have ever found them the meanest and basest, the most cruel and cowardly, of all others. It was my unhappy lot not only to belong to a religious slaveholder, but to live in a community of such religionists. (82)

This passage, taken together with the whole of chapter 9 and the appendix to the *Narrative*, in which Douglass specifies his critique of religion as that of "slave holding religion," stands as testament to the centrality of religion as one of the main discursive issues for abolitionists even by the mid–nineteenth century. This clearly continued to be the case some fifteen years later, near the dawning of the Civil War. Martin Delaney's protagonist Henry, in *Blake; or, The Huts of America* (1859–61), utters these words to his revolutionary compatriots, who are in the process of plotting a rebellion:

> "You must make your religion subserve your interest, as your oppressors do theirs!" advised Henry. "They use the Scriptures to make you submit, by preaching to you the texts of 'obedience to your masters' and 'standing still to see the salvation,' and we must now begin to understand the Bible so as to make it of interest to us."[6]

And if we are to trust Delaney's representation in the novel of Henry's revolutionary attitude toward religion as being in generational conflict with the old slave Mammy Judy (who believed that slaves must simply "trust in the Lord"), it stands to reason that Douglass may also have been addressing himself to this kind of complexity in attitudes about religion. Chiefly, it demonstrates his recognition of the importance of religion to the discursive reader of his narrative, especially as Christianity's moral sanction was something to which both abolitionists and pro-slavery advocates wanted to lay claim.

Clearly, the climax of Douglass's philosophical critique of slavery, and the longest chapter in the *Narrative*, is chapter 10. Its narrative trajectory brings together many of the strands that Douglass discusses throughout his text, including his now-classic battle with Mr. Covey; his meditation on the "whole system of fraud and inhumanity of slavery" (especially his very interesting reading of the masters' use of the Christian holidays in relation to the slaves); his discussion of how slavery prevents the cultivation of the slave's mind and spirit; his joy at holding a "Sabbath school," where he taught other slaves to read; his plot to escape with a few of his fellow slaves; his ill treatment, with no redress, at the hands of Mr. Gardner's men; and his understanding of the economics of slavery, which necessitated that he turn over his wages at the end of each week to his master. In this most narratively unwieldy chapter of his account, Douglass brings together for the benefit of his reader the many concerns he addresses about slavery.

Still, the most striking aspect of this chapter is how it displays the caprice and randomness of corporal punishment of slaves by their masters. Douglass especially links the severity of this kind of behavior to the more religious of the slaveholders. The accounts show the psychological terror under which slaves existed. They also bear witness to the aspect of the discursive reader that lacks a proximate understanding of slavery, by reinforcing and legitimating what white abolitionists have been saying about the brutalities of slavery, even as it further discredits pro-slavery advocates' image of the happy slave: "It would astonish one, unaccustomed to a slaveholding life, to see with what wonderful ease a slaveholder can find things, of which to make occasion to whip slaves" (82). This statement to the reader who has a distant understanding of slavery further signals Douglass's purposefulness of address. Douglass not only understands his discursive reader but fashions his testimony with this reader's concerns in mind.

The confluence of interests that Douglass brings together in chapter 10, along with the other moments I have examined here, demonstrates the extent to which he is attentive to these narrative pressures.

Any testimony that is to be successful—by which I mean in this context, that is to have political efficacy for the cause of abolitionism—must address itself, as I said in chapter 1, to the very discourse that creates, allows, and enables the situation for the slave to be able to speak to us at all. It must recognize the codes and terms that animate abolitionist discourse. By examining Douglass's *Narrative* in light of its discursive reader, we come to appreciate what it means to successfully negotiate these terms. And no more successful slave testimony could be found than that of Douglass. I dare say that the amount of critical attention it has continued to garner, even among contemporary students of the African American slave-narrative tradition, further testifies to its complexity and subtlety in addressing itself to the irksome overdeterminacies of abolitionist discourse.

# AFTERWORD

The work of *Impossible Witnesses* has interested me in its specificity, but it has also fascinated me for the paradigmatic possibilities it offers up. The suggestions in this book for understanding slave testimony may also be paradigmatically helpful in our efforts to appreciate more fully our contemporary political climate and the issues of, say, affirmative action or gay and lesbian rights. It is evident to those of us living in the present moment that these issues are linked to people's contesting understandings of "equality," for example. It is clear that affirmative action, thanks to the rhetorical savvy of the political right, is today seen by many as "reverse discrimination" (an idea that could scarcely have been imagined in 1960s America). It is also clear that many now argue against affirmative action on the grounds of its negative effects on the self-esteem of the minorities it is designed to benefit. And we know that even though white women have been the greatest overall beneficiaries of affirmative action, they are also the least often discussed in the public debates over these policies.

By the same token, we know that the supposed Christian immorality of homosexuality is one of the chief reasons that the political right is opposed to gay and lesbian rights. We are aware of the way in which the language of "family" and "family values" has been used as a means of censoring certain cultural productions with queer content, and of how the political right has tried to make family into their own ideological domain, to which gays and lesbians have no access. We are also aware of the ways in which the gay and lesbian community has taken on that language of family and insisted that it describes our families as much as it does those of our heterosexual counterparts. And since these contestations have made unlikely political allies of gays and lesbians and heterosexual single parents (particularly single mothers), the situation attests to the truth value of the old adage about politics and strange bedfellows. Again, we are well aware that these are complex, highly contested issues in our time. Still, some one hundred years hence, scholars will be puzzling over the number of books and the amount of public debate during this *fin-de-siècle* surrounding these, hopefully by then antiquated issues of sexuality and affirmative action. When they do, we can only hope that they will look back and see—as we have come to see with the abolitionists—that in order to construct as clear a picture as possible of what these texts represented in their time, one must first reconstruct, as best one can, the discursive milieu to which the work was addressing itself. By that I do not mean a mere statement of the historical facts (which in the case of abolitionism are well documented by scores of historians), but rather an attention to the historicity of discourses themselves, which takes stock of the attitudes of the time and of their interrelations with testimonial texts.

I have tried, throughout this book, to point out the character and extent of abolitionist discourse and the cultural milieu out of which it sprang. I have also tried to show the need this discursive milieu had for slave testimony. And I have endeavored to demonstrate some of the rhetorical strategies that slave witnesses had to employ in order to navigate this discursive terrain and to tell their "truth" about slavery. Finally, I have tried to demonstrate the need to listen anew to these slave witnesses, with our attention focused on abolitionist discourse as a living entity, functioning as a discursive reader that both limits and enables the occasion for slave testimony. When read in this way, not only do the impact and complexity of abolitionist discourse come into clearer focus, but we also witness what it means to tell the "truth" about slavery come closer to being both heard and understood.

# NOTES

1. Thomas Gossett, in *Race: The History of an Idea,* reports that Darwin's theory of evolution excited a movement which was already a major concern of many nineteenth-century anthropologists—the measurement of race differences. The search for such differences has been described by Ruth Benedict in *Race: Science and Politics.* Gossett also tells us that the eighteenth-century idea of a correlation between color and climate was challenged in Europe by Peter Simon Pallas as early as 1780. Even so, the idea continued to have currency in the discourse on race well into the nineteenth century. See chapters 3, 4, and 7 in Gossett.

2. This book's empahsis on the dynamics of power between the slave and the master and between the slave and his/her reader demonstrates the extent to which this work participates in what Lindon Barrett identifies as the "[attentiveness of] cultural studies to the exigencies of power and powerlessness and their subtle, pervasive insinuations" (Barrett, 3).

3. My understanding of Foucault is informed by specific texts by Foucault as well as select secondary readings. Primary references include but are not limited to: *Discipline and Punish, The Archeology of Knowledge,* and *The Order of Things.* The commentators that I rely on most heavily include but are not limited to: Paul Bové, Gilles Deleuze, Charles Taylor, Jon Simons, Herbert Dreyfus, and Paul Rabinow. I try to outline a way of theorizing the necessity for certain kinds of rhetorical strategizing and essentializing, given the restrictive discourses in which the speech act of the slave takes place. In brief, the slave has to make use of restrictive discourses that overdetermine, fix, and subject the terms available to the slave in order to describe or tell his or her story. If the only truth available is the truth enabled by the limits of the same restrictive discourses that subjugate, what, then, are the possibilities for resistance? The analysis in each of the subsequent chapters supports a hypothesis that tries to answer this question. For a further discussion of the problem of representation as it might relate to the issue of witnessing as I discuss it here, see also Gayatri Spivak's famous essay "Can the Subaltern Speak?."

4. George Riley Scott, in *The History of Torture,* makes the distinction between penal and private punishments. For him, penal punishments are public and prescribed by law. Private punishments cover the various other kinds of beatings or torture that are not prescribed by law. This category of private punishments, for my purposes, would include what I am here calling the nature of corporal punishment, in that it was often conducted

purposely in the view of other slaves (as described by slave narrators) so as to function as a kind of negative conditioning. On the issue of the auction block, Mary Prince's description of herself and her family on the auction block provides an interesting example of the staging of slavery. And all this still does not begin to account for the numerous images in the visual arts of the period that have been underanalyzed in terms of their participation in spectacularizing slavery.

5. For a broader discussion of the spectacle and the spectacularizing of slavery, see Saidya Hartman's *Scenes of Subjection: Terror, Slavery, and Self-Making in Nineteenth-Century America* (especially chapter 1, "Innocent Amusements: The Stage of Suffrance") and Joseph Roach's 1992 essay, "Slave Spectacles and Tragic Octoroons: A Cultural Genealogy of Antebellum Performance."

6. Henry Louis Gates, Jr., and Charles Davis tell us that these narratives were often spoken or performed publicly many times by the narrators before they were ever committed in writing.

7. Prince's anthropomorphizing of the house might also be linked with a similar idea circulating in Romantic thought, expressed best by William Blake in his poem "Auguries of Innocence," which begins:

> To see a World in a Grain of Sand
> And a Heaven in a Wild Flower
> Hold Infinity in the palm of your hand
> And Eternity in an hour

This is suggestive of one tenet of Romantic thought—that there is life and divinity in everything in nature. In a longer treatment of this particular issue, it might be interesting to discover how this idea is deformed by slavery, and how slave witnesses make use of this deformation of the Romantic ideal.

8. For a more extended discussion of slavery as primarily a shared condition, see Howard McGary and Bill E. Lawson's *Between Slavery and Freedom.*

9. For a discussion of this idea of "hidden transcripts," see James Scott's *Domination and the Arts of Resistance.* Frederick Douglass, among others, provides excellent examples in *Narrative of the Life of Frederick Douglass* of how slaves act and speak in the slave community versus how they perform in the presence of white masters.

10. This list includes, but is not limited to, such representative figures as Emerson, Fuller, and Garrison, alongside Blake, Edgeworth, and Cowper.

11. As *Impossible Witnesses* was being prepared for press, Helen Thomas's excellent study *Romanticism and Slave Narratives: Transatlantic Testimonies* was

published. Regrettably, I did not have an opportunity to engage meaningfully with her work in this book.

12. Robert Stepto, among others, has made compelling contributions to the study of the issues of authenticity surrounding this narrative.

13. I am not the first to suggest how central and useful the work of Bakhtin has been to African American literary analysis. One of the most recent scholars to put forward that centrality is Katherine Clay Bassard, in her 1999 book, *Spiritual Interrogations: Culture, Gender, and Community in Early African American Women's Writing.*

NOTES TO CHAPTER 2

1. The trend in the scholarship is changing in recent years. More work has appeared in the last decade of the twentieth century that recognizes the importance of complicating received notions of "canon" that make large, sweeping claims about the character of the literature of an entire period. Consider the exemplary work of Eric Sundquist in *To Wake the Nations: Race in the Making of American Literature* and Toni Morrison's *Playing in the Dark: Whiteness and the Literary Imagination* and her essay "Unspeakable Things Unspoken." I think here also of Anne K. Mellor's *Romanticism and Gender,* Alan Richardson and Sonia Hofkosh's edited book *Romanticism, Race, and Imperial Culture;* the anthology edited by Anne Mellor and Richard E. Matlak, *British Literature, 1780–1830,* which is a significant revision of the Romantic canon from that of David Perkins's earlier standard *English Romantic Writers;* and Helen Thomas's book *Romanticism and Slave Narratives: Transatlantic Testimonies,* which was published as *Impossible Witnesses* was going to press.

2. A year later, in 1788, La Société des Amis des Noirs was formed in Paris with the support of the British society. They were in correspondence with each other even in those early days. Evidence of this comes in the form of the letters of Condorcet, a founder of La Société.

3. Emerson's important essay "Nature" was published in 1836.

4. All translations in this book, unless otherwise noted, are my own.

5. Paine had also been outspoken about the atrocities of Britain in Africa, India, and the Caribbean.

6. *Rights of Man* is both a political-philosophical defense of the French Revolution and a challenge to England to revolutionize its own aristocratic system. It should also be noted that, in 1792, Paine was chosen as a delegate to the French National Convention. And despite his not being a francophone, the new French Republic also appointed Paine to the Committee of Nine to frame the new constitution.

7. I am aware of William James's unpublished dissertation from UCLA, "The Black Man in English Romantic Literature, 1772–1833," and the study done by Eva Beatrice Dykes, *The Negro in English Romantic Thought, or A Study of Sympathy for the Oppressed.* Dykes's text is an excellent cataloging of the writers who mentioned Blacks in their text or who referred to their plight. It is an early groundbreaking study, however, and as such it does not make the kinds of distinctions among these mentions that one would like. All mentions of Blacks are accorded equal status in Dykes's text. I want to discern more of the larger discourses of subjugation and power that these specific utterances rely on, participate in, and, indeed, help create and extend.

8. See chapter 1 of Marilyn Gaull's *English Romanticism: The Human Context* for these and other issues that would have been popular concerns of the Romantics in the English context.

9. In *Romanticism and Gender*, Mellor focuses on four dimensions of what she labels "revolutionary feminine Romanticism," of which she positions Mary Wollstonecraft as the primary progenitor: "the education of the rational woman, rational love and the politics of domestic responsibility, women's relation to nature, and the feminine construction of subjectivity" (39).

10. See Davis and Gates's *The Slave's Narrative.*

11. Further testament to the transatlantic intertextuality of the period comes in the epigraph from Byron that Duras assigns to *Ourika*: "This is to be alone, this, this is solitude!" This also echoes one of the traditional tropes of Romanticism—solitude, aloneness, the individual standing apart from society. For different valences of this issue of transatlantic intertextuality, see also Jennifer DeVere Brody's *Impossible Purities: Blackness, Femininity, and Victorian Culture* (1998) and David Brion Davis's classic work *The Problem of Slavery in Western Culture* (1966).

12. From "The Mansfield Judgement," in *British Literature, 1780–1830*, ed. Anne K. Mellor and Richard E. Matlak (57). For an engaging rendering of the history of the Somerset case, see Gretchen Gerzina's *Black London: Life before Emancipation* (1995).

13. Quoted in Howard Temperley, *British Antislavery, 1833–1870*, 1.

14. See Robert J. Allison, "Introduction: Equiano's Worlds," in Olaudah Equiano's *The Interesting Narrative of the Life of Olaudah Equiano, Written by Himself*, 10–12.

15. The Meeting for Sufferings developed from the groups that Quakers had formed much earlier in the eighteenth century in order to prevent the persecution of Quakers themselves.

16. This David Hartley is not to be confused with the notable eighteenth-

century English philosopher, who died in 1758. Rather, this is David Hartley, Esq., and member of the Parliament of Great Britain. This is the Hartley who was appointed by the Crown to sign the Paris Treaty for Britain in 1783, ending the American Revolutionary War and ceding the Northwest Territory to the United States.

17. Vincent Newey, "The Abolition of the Slave Trade," in *A Handbook to British Romanticism*, ed. Jean Raimond and J. R. Watson, 1.

18. See Paul Johnson's *A History of the American People* (1997) and Daniel C. Littlefield's "Revolutionary Citizens: 1776–1804," in *To Make Our World Anew: A History of African Americans*, ed. Robin D. G. Kelley and Earl Lewis (2000).

19. See James Clyde Sellman's article "Abolitionism in the United States" at http://www.Africana.com.

20. See Benezet's most well-known work, *Some Historical Account of Guinea* (1771).

21. Benezet's arguments here are the ones from which Equiano borrows in his narrative to make his moral argument against slavery and even to suggest the moral superiority of Africans over Europeans. I discuss this in some detail in chapter 5.

22. C. Duncan Rice, *The Rise and Fall of Black Slavery*, 153.

23. For a broader discussion of this idea of class sensibility, see Thomas L. Haskell's "Capitalism and the Origins of the Humanitarian Sensibility, Part 1" and "Capitalism and the Origins of the Humanitarian Sensibility, Part 2."

24. For more information, see *Extracts from the Evidence Taken before Committees of the Two Houses of Parliament Relative to the Slave Trade, with Illustrations from Collateral Sources*.

25. For more detail on these kinds of demographics, see Higman's extremely thorough study *Slave Populations of the British Caribbean, 1807–1834*.

26. For a more detailed description of the instances of torture to which the slaves were subjected, see George Riley Scott's *The History of Torture*.

27. George Stephen, *Antislavery Recollections*, 159–60.

28. Clare Midgley, *Women against Slavery: The British Campaigns, 1780–1870*, 34–35.

29. See George E. Boulukos's excellent 1999 published essay, "Maria Edgeworth's 'Grateful Negro' and the Sentimental Argument for Slavery," both for how he locates her in her historical context and for how he defines her moral position on slavery as one that is in between the radical anti-slavery possibilities and the pro-slavery possibilities available to her.

30. Maria Edgeworth, "The Grateful Negro," in *British Literature, 1780–*

*1830*, ed. Anne K. Mellor and Richard E. Matlak, 549. All further reference to this text is made parenthetically in the text.

31. This should remind the reader of a good American analogue to this story, *The Confessions of Nat Turner*. Turner's position is one of righteous indignation against all whites that operates exclusively within a politics of institution.

32. This should be read as an allusion to natural rights discourse, the idea that humankind everywhere is born free and equal. Rousseau, as I discuss in chapter 4, argues in his *Discourse on the Origins of Inequality* that only the differences of time and location give rise to inequality.

33. William Cowper, "The Negro's Complaint," in *British Literature, 1780–1830*, ed. Anne K. Mellor and Richard E. Matlak, 62.

34. Amelia Alderson Opie, "The Black Man's Lament, or, How to Make Sugar," in *British Literature, 1780–1830*, ed. Anne K. Mellor and Richard E. Matlak, 84.

35. This reading is informed by the reference to "sun-burnt face" in line 15. The idea that Africans' color was a result of overexposure to sunlight, due to the geographical locales from which they were brought, was a popular climatological theory in the eighteenth century. This being referred to specifically later in the poem allows us to think of the present reference in a different way.

36. Albert J. Raboteau, *Slave Religion*, 290, states: "The tendency of Christianity to support the established order has long been noted and criticized by some. It has been alleged that Christianity, with its other-worldly, compensatory emphasis, is a religion particularly fitted for slaves."

37. It should be noted that the view of being in the presence of God here articulated by the speaker is mediated by his positionality in this world, the fallen world. Hence, all the musings on the otherworldly are finally speculative.

38. Leopold Damrosch, *Symbol and Truth in Blake's Myth*, 151.

39. The problem with the desire for "likeness" here is that it implicitly relies on a hierarchy or an hegemony of whiteness over blackness.

40. Lorenzo D. Turner, *Anti-Slavery Sentiment in American Literature prior to 1865*, 3.

41. See "Garrison, William Lloyd," in *The Historical Encyclopedia of World Slavery, Volume One*, 297. *The Liberator* did not cease its publication until the Thirteenth Amendment to the Constitution was passed, abolishing slavery.

42. Garner's story is one of a fugitive slave who attempted to kill herself and her three children (she was successful in killing one of them).

The occasion was her being found by her former master, who planned to take not only her but her children (who were born in the free North) back into slavery. Her hatred and fear of slavery was so strong that she opted for infanticide. This is related in a newspaper clipping in Middleton Harris's *The Black Book.*

43. For a fuller explanation of the context of Reconstruction, see John Hope Franklin, *From Slavery to Freedom,* 293–328 and chapters 5 and 6 of Robin D. G. Kelley and Earl Lewis's *To Make Our World Anew.*

44. August Meier, *Negro Thought in America, 1880–1915,* 19.

45. These states literally incorporated disenfranchisement provisions into their constitutions, according to Meier.

46. David Brion Davis, *The Problem of Slavery in Western Culture,* 25.

47. Hereafter referred to as "The Address."

48. Ralph Waldo Emerson, "The Fugitive Slave Law," in *The Portable Emerson,* ed. Carl Bode, 548. All further references to this text are made parenthetically in the text.

49. Barbara Johnson, "Response" [to H. L. Gates, Jr.'s "Canon-Formation and the Afro-American Tradition"], in *Afro-American Literary Study in the 1990's,* ed. Houston A. Baker, Jr., and Patricia Redmond, 43.

50. Whigs in mid-nineteenth-century America were still connected to commercial progressivism, as they were in England. This was especially the case after the Jackson presidency, which led the nation down the path of financial crisis and into an eventual depression. See Paul Johnson's discussion of the politics between the Whigs and the Democrats of this period in *A History of the American People* (especially 352–59).

51. In terms of his implied critique of economic greed on the part of whites associated with slavery, Emerson's views are on a continuum with those of David Walker in the *Appeal.* Sterling Stuckey reminds us, in his discussion of Walker's view of whites, that "the essence of European character was for Walker a desire for power linked to an insatiable love of gain" (*Slave Culture,* 121).

52. What would be worth unpacking, among other things, in a longer treatment is the problem of how white male subjectivity is both negatively impacted by and dependent on the existence of the slave. Hegel would be sufficient to open up such a discussion.

53. He cites Hume and Jefferson, among others.

54. In all fairness to Fuller, it should be noted that her use of whiteness may be a rhetorical device employed in order to avoid alienating her audience. This reading could be sustained by an examination of her passage on William Lloyd Garrison and his inability to speak in "a key agreeable to common ears."

55. See Sterling Stuckey's account of Walker's death and of its impact, in *Slave Culture*, 136–37.

56. Truman Nelson, ed., *Documents of Upheaval: Selections from William Lloyd Garrison's* The Liberator, *1831–1865*, 4. All further citations from *The Liberator* are taken from this volume and are cited parenthetically in the text.

57. Lundy, born in New Jersey of Quaker parents, was a pioneer in American anti-slavery. He formed his own anti-slavery organization while working in Ohio in 1815, and in 1821 he launched the *Genius of Universal Emancipation*, a periodical devoted to anti-slavery reporting and writing. In 1829, Garrison became the associate editor of the paper. The men parted ways, however, over the issue of African slave colonization from the United States, which Lundy supported and Garrison did not. For more information on Lundy, see Thomas Earle's *The Life, Travels and Opinions of Benjamin Lundy* (1847).

58. Garrison's rhetorical move here points up one of the discursive regularities of abolitionism. That is, Garrison's rhetoric in this instance seems to recognize that aspect of racialized discourse which necessitates the appeal to what we might call, in today's literary theoretical terms, after Gayatri Spivak, a "strategic essentialism." See Spivak's *The Post-Colonial Critic* (1990).

59. A familiar trend to observe in slavery debates is that each time there was an insurrection or an inflammatory tract such as this one was published, pro-slavery advocates quickly moved to hold abolitionists responsible. This strategy is also telling because it assumes that Africans themselves cannot possibly have such thoughts on their own. Again, Africans' minds, bodies, and humanity are ever sites of contestation.

60. Of the first 450 subscribers to *The Liberator*, 400 were free blacks.

61. In this regard, Garrison's tendency to blame whites for the creation of black rage is not unlike Walker's own militant logic in the *Appeal.*

NOTES TO CHAPTER 3

1. See Mary Prince, *The History of Mary Prince: A West Indian Slave. Related by Herself.* ed. Moira Ferguson. All further references to this book are made parenthetically in the text. Critics who have commented on Prince include William L. Andrews, in *Black Women's Slave Narratives*; Henry Louis Gates, Jr., in his brief introduction to *The Classic Slave Narratives*, in which Prince's narrative is included; Moira Ferguson, in *Subject to Others*; and Jenny Sharpe, in "'Something Akin to Freedom': The Case of Mary Prince."

2. Moira Ferguson, *Subject to Others: British Women Writers and Colonial*

*Slavery, 1670–1834*, 283. All further references to this text will be made parenthetically in the text.

3. Henry Louis Gates, Jr., "Introduction," in *The Classic Slave Narratives*, ed. Henry Louis Gates, Jr., xv.

4. Quoted in Gates's introduction to *The Classic Slave Narrative*, xvi.

5. Such logic prefigures, if in a somewhat vulgar way, Nietzsche's later understanding in *Toward a Genealogy of Morals* of "slave morality" as fundamentally problematic. In a longer study this would bear more consideration. Nietzsche describes it this way: "The slave's revolt in morals begins with this, that *ressentiment* itself becomes creative and gives birth to values: the *ressentiment* of those who are denied the real reaction, that of the deed, and who compensate with an imaginary revenge. Whereas all noble morality grows out of a triumphant affirmation of oneself, slave morality immediately says No to what comes from outside, to what is different, to what is not oneself: and *this* No is the creative deed. This reversal of the value-posting glance—this *necessary* direction outward instead of back to oneself—is of the nature of *ressentiment*: to come into being, slave morality requires an outside world, a counterworld; physiologically speaking, it requires external stimuli in order to react at all: its action is at bottom always a reaction" (451). See *The Portable Nietzsche*, ed. Walter Kaufmann (New York: Penguin, 1982).

6. The references Prince makes to the good people of England in the narrative should not go without comment. This representation of people in England as "good," as opposed to their countrymen in the colonies, is a familiar rhetorical tactic of abolitionist discourse in Britain.

7. The idea of the "discursive reader" receives only brief articulation here but is addressed more fully in chapter 6. What I mean, in brief, by this idea (a fusion of Foucault's ideas on "discursive formations" and Bakhtin's "dialogism") is that there are certain forces, with which she is always in dialogue, that cause Prince to feel the need to authenticate herself. She is not addressing a particular group of individuals or a particular audience but rather the discursive parameters that constitute the racialist discourse of slavery (debates over African humanity, inferiority, morality, work ethics, etc.).

8. An interesting theoretical analogue of this problem of experience, time, and narrative is addressed in the director Kathryn Bigelow's 1995 film *Strange Days* (20th Century Fox). Through a new technology, one can relive moments that another has lived, from his or her vantage point. But even in this scenario, time prevents one from actually being there. Since one is living a moment already lived, there is no responsibility in the moment or to the moment. And there is always the option of checking out when one likes.

The technology becomes a black market "drug" to which people become addicted, thus reinscribing the fetish value of the experience of the other.

9. See my discussion of Margaret Fuller and of this quote in chapter 2, in the section on Fuller's review of Douglass's *Narrative*.

10. "Verifiable" here means verifiable through various attestations, letters, corroborating white witnesses, narrative detail, and, finally, the slave's body itself.

11. See James Olney's essay "'I Was Born': Slave Narratives, Their Status as Autobiography and as Literature," in *The Slave's Narrative*, ed. Charles T. Davis and Henry Louis Gates, Jr., 165–66.

## NOTES TO CHAPTER 4

1. By "testimonial moments," I mean those passages in the text that appear to be aware of themselves as testimonial, aware of the discursive situation in which they are participating, and often even preoccupied with providing evidence for their own political cause.

2. Seymour Gross, "Introduction: Stereotype to the Archetype: The Negro in American Literary Criticism," in *Images of the Negro in American Literature*, 3.

3. J. Saunders Redding, *To Make a Poet Black*, 11.

4. William H. Robinson, *Phillis Wheatley in the Black American Beginnings*, 28.

5. See, for example, Moira Ferguson's *Subject to Others*, especially chapter 6; Betsy Erkkila's "Revolutionary Women"; Henry Louis Gates, Jr.'s *Figures in Black*; Russell J. Reising's *Loose Ends*; James A. Levernier's "Phillis Wheatley and the New England Clergy"; Walt Nott's "From 'Uncultivated Barbarian' to 'Poetical Genius': The Public Presence of Phillis Wheatley"; Hilene Flanzbaum's "Unprecedented Liberties: Re-reading Phillis Wheatley"; and Robert Reid-Pharr's introduction to his *Conjugal Union*.

6. Robinson, *Phillis Wheatley*, 13.

7. Margaret Matilda Odell, "Memoir," in *Phillis Wheatley and Her Writings*, ed. William H. Robinson (New York: Garland, 1984), 430.

8. Robinson, *Phillis Wheatley*, 13.

9. Ibid., 14.

10. Ibid., 15.

11. Henry Louis Gates, Jr., "Foreword: In Her Own Write," in *The Collected Works of Phillis Wheatley*, ed. John C. Shields, viii.

12. Henry Louis Gates, "Introduction: 'Race' Writing and the Difference It Makes," in *"Race," Writing and Difference*, ed. Henry Louis Gates, 8.

13. It is true that "slaves" and "servants" are not the same. However, the

rhetorical use to which the biblical language of "servants" was put in the context of slavery is well documented by Albert J. Raboteau in *Slave Religion: The "Invisible Institution" in the Antebellum South.*

14. For a treatment of this use of scriptural authority well into the nineteenth century (even leading up to the Civil War), see Albert Raboteau's *Slave Religion: The "Invisible Institution" in the Antebellum South*, especially chapter 5.

15. Robinson, *Phillis Wheatley*, 30.

16. Ibid., 42.

17. John Shields, in Phillis Wheatley, *The Collected Works of Phillis Wheatley*, ed. John Shields, 229.

18. Gates, *"Race,"* 7–8.

19. Redding, *To Make a Poet Black*, 12.

20. Angelene Jamison, "Analysis of Selected Poetry of Phillis Wheatley," in *Critical Essays on Phillis Wheatley*, ed. William H. Robinson, 128.

21. Redding, *To Make a Poet Black*, 13.

22. Robinson, *Phillis Wheatley*, 38.

23. Phillis Wheatley, *The Collected Works of Phillis Wheatley*, ed. John Shields. All further reference to Wheatley's are from this edition.

24. June Jordan, "The Difficult Miracle of Black Poetry in America," 255.

25. It is interesting to note here also how the "good" that Wheatley imagines God will turn Africans into is rendered in exclusively masculine terms.

26. This investigation of the idea of hierarchy of persons under God harks back at least as far as John Winthrop's sermon "A Modell of Christian Charity" (first delivered in 1630 aboard the *Arabella*).

27. John Shields, "Phillis Wheatley's Struggle for Freedom," in Phillis Wheatley, *The Collected Works of Phillis Wheatley*, ed. John Shields, 238.

28. Phillis Wheatley, "To the Rev. Samuel Hopkins," 9 February 1774, letter in *The Collected Works of Phillis Wheatley*, ed. John Shields, 175.

29. Phillis Wheatley, "To Rev. Samson Occom," 11 February 1774, letter in *Phillis Wheatley and Her Writings*, ed. William H. Robinson (New York: Garland, 1984), 332.

30. According to William Robinson, this letter was published first in the *Connecticut Gazette* (March 11, 1774) and later in the *Massachusetts Spy* (March 24, 1774). This letter, Robinson adds, went on to be printed in over a dozen New England newspapers.

NOTES TO CHAPTER 5

1. Hereafter I refer to Equiano's narrative as *Life*.

2. This passage should be recalled later, when there is a more extended

discussion of this issue of complexion in relationship to Jefferson's use of it in *Notes on the State of Virginia*.

3. See Keith A. Sandiford, *Measuring the Moment: Strategies of Protest in Eighteenth-Century Afro-English Writing*; and Angelo Costanzo, *Surprising Narrative: Olaudah Equiano and the Beginnings of Black Autobiography*.

4. See chapter 1 of Houston A. Baker, *Blues, Ideology, and Afro-American Literature: A Vernacular Theory*.

5. Joseph Fichtelberg, "Words between Worlds: The Economy of Equiano's Narrative," 461.

6. For a good treatment of the critical legacy of the slave narrative, see Jennifer Fleishner's "Introduction" in *Mastering Slavery* (New York: New York University Press, 1996), 11–32.

7. Thomas Jefferson, *Notes on the State of Virginia*, ed. William Peden. All further reference to this work is from this edition and is made parenthetically in the text.

8. See Robert Allison, "Introduction: Equiano's World," in Olaudah Equiano, *The Interesting Narrative of the Life of Olaudah Equiano*, ed. Robert Allison, 1–26; and Angelo Costanzo, *Surprising Narrative: Olaudah Equiano and the Beginnings of Black Autobiography*.

9. Katalin Orban, "Dominant and Submerged Discourses in *The Life of Olaudah Equiano* (or Gustavus Vassa?)," 655.

10. Olaudah Equiano, *The Interesting Narrative of the Life of Olaudah Equiano, or Gustavus Vassa, the African. Written by Himself*, in *The Classic Slave Narratives*, ed. Henry Louis Gates, Jr., 11. All further citations to Equiano's narrative are from this edition and are provided parenthetically in the text. Quotations from Allison refer to his introduction to the Bedford edition.

11. Since the writing of this chapter, critic Vincent Carretta has persuasively argued that Equiano was not, in fact, born in Africa but in the American South. (See Carretta's 1999 essay "Olaudah Equiano or Gustavus Vassa?: New Light on an Eighteenth-Century Question of Identity.") If Carretta is right—and indeed, his argument is based on fairly unassailable primary document research—then this dramatizes even more the point I go on to make here about how Equiano strategically uses his rather romantic representation of Africa in both his moral critique of slavery and his argument for African moral superiority over Europeans. In fact, Carretta's essay takes the already-vexed issue of witnessing and adds yet another layer of complexity to it. Consider the moment when, in another context, Betsy Erkkila, while glossing the "historicity of literature," poses the following set of somewhat rhetorical questions to remind us of the different meanings of "literature" in the eighteenth century: "Is the Declaration of Independence fact or fiction? Is Benjamin Franklin's *Autobiography* history or literature? Is *The Interesting Narrative of the Life of Olaudah Equiano, or Gustavus Vassa, The*

*African* truth or fiction?" ("A Critical History," *American Quarterly* 50, 2 [1998]: 361). Just as Erkkila invites us to think about the historicity of literature, we might take Carretta as an opportunity to ruminate on the historicity of "truth."

I have been arguing throughout this book the difference between actual slave experience and the narrative or testimonial truth of slavery. If we understand truth as always a production, a process, a political operation, then what matters most to the work at hand is the attention we pay to the rhetorical strategies enacted to produce truth. If Carretta is right, and Equiano was not born in Africa, we must then pursue the question, as we do here, of what Equiano gains from fabricating that part of his past. Put another way, the answer to Erkkila's question with regard to whether Equiano's narrative is truth or fiction is that it does not matter. What matters is why he wanted he readers to believe that truth, and how he achieved its narrative representation.

12. The much later critique of Jefferson's *Notes* in David Walker's *Appeal* (1831) further signifies the persistence of the cultural centrality of Jefferson's thought with regard to the argument for African inferiority.

13. This is also the passage from which David Walker quotes in the *Appeal.*

14. Will Durant, *The Story of Philosophy*, 407.

15. See chapter 3 of Shoshana Felman and Dori Laub, *Testimony: Crises of Witnessing in Literature, Psychoanalysis, and History*, where Laub quotes a woman survivor from the Yale Holocaust Video Archive stating the following: "We wanted to survive so as to live one day after Hitler, in order to be able to tell our story" (78).

16. Felman and Laub, *Testimony: Crises of Witnessing in Literature, Psychoanalysis, and History*, 42–44.

17. See Cornel West, *Race Matters*, especially chapter 1.

18. See Jean-Jacques Rousseau, "Discourse on the Origin and Basis of Inequality among Men," in *The Essential Rousseau*, trans. Lowell Bair, 125–201. Rousseau states the following:

> It is easy to see that if we are to discover the origin of the differences that now exist among men, we must seek it in those successive changes in the human constitution. . . . Such was the first source of inequality among men. (138)

Equiano follows this logic in his earlier Edenic, pastoral representations of his homeland and, later, when he argues that Africans have not had the opportunity to improve themselves in the way Europeans have. This does not, to his mind, make Africans inferior, however.

19. Luke 4:16–21, King James Version.

20. In Equiano's words, slavery "violates the first natural right of mankind, equality and independency" (80).

21. The use of "your" here provides further evidence that the audience being addressed in this specific instance is an audience of white planters.

## NOTES TO CHAPTER 6

1. Benedict Anderson, *Imagined Communities: Reflections on the Origin and Spread of Nationalism*, rev. ed. (London and New York: Verso, 1993). See especially the "Introduction."

2. David W. Blight, "Introduction: 'A Psalm of Freedom,'" in *Narrative of the Life of Frederick Douglass, An American Slave: Written by Himself*, ed. David W. Blight, 16.

3. Recall the earlier footnoted discussion in chapter 5 on whether Equiano's narrative is true in terms of how he represents himself as a native African.

4. This moment in particular from Douglass's narrative has been taken up most recently, and most provocatively, perhaps, in Saidya Hartman's *Scenes of Subjection: Terror, Slavery, and Self-Making in Nineteenth Century America*. Hartman writes:

The "terrible spectacle" that introduced Frederick Douglass to slavery was the beating of his Aunt Hester. It is one of the most well-known scenes of torture in the literature of slavery, perhaps second only to Uncle Tom's murder at the hands of Simon Legree. By locating this "horrible exhibition" in the first chapter of his 1845 *Narrative of the Life of Frederick Douglass*, Douglass establishes the centrality of violence to the making of the slave and identifies it as an original generative act equivalent to the statement "I was born." The passage through the blood-stained gate is an inaugural moment in the formation of the enslaved. In this regard, it is a primal scene. By this I mean that the terrible spectacle dramatizes the origin of the subject and demonstrates that to be a slave is to be under the brutal power and authority of another; this is confirmed by the event's placement in the opening chapter on genealogy. (3)

5. See my essay "Speaking the Unspeakable: On Toni Morrison, African American Intellectuals and the Uses of Essentialist Rhetoric," in *Reading Toni Morrison: Theoretical and Critical Approaches*, ed. Nancy J. Peterson, 131–52.

6. See Martin R. Delaney, *Blake; or, The Huts of America*, 41.

# BIBLIOGRAPHY

Abrams, M. H. *The Mirror and the Lamp: Romantic Theory and the Critical Tradition.* Oxford and New York: Oxford University Press, 1953.

Allen, Theodore W. *The Invention of the White Race: Racial Oppression and Social Control.* Vol. 1. London and New York: Verso, 1994.

Allison, Robert. "Introduction: Equiano's Worlds." In Olaudah Equiano, *The Interesting Narrative of the Life of Olaudah Equiano or Gustavus Vassa, the African. Written by Himself,* ed. Robert J. Allison. Boston and New York: Bedford, 1995: 1–26.

Andrews, William, ed. *Black Women's Slave Narratives.* New York: Oxford University Press, 1987.

———. *To Tell a Free Story: The First Century of Afro-American Autobiography, 1760–1865.* Urbana: University of Illinois Press, 1986.

Apter, Emily. *Feminizing the Fetish: Psychoanalysis and Narrative Obsession in Turn-of-the-Century France.* Ithaca and London: Cornell University Press, 1991.

Aptheker, Herbert. *Abolitionism: A Revolutionary Movement.* Boston: Twayne, 1989.

Arac, Jonathan, ed. *After Foucault: Humanistic Knowledge, Postmodern Challenges.* New Brunswick, NJ: Rutgers University Press, 1991.

Bailyn, Bernard. *Voyagers to the West: A Passage in the Peopling of America on the Eve of the Revolution.* New York: Knopf, 1986.

Baker, Houston A., Jr. *Blues, Ideology, and Afro-American Literature: A Vernacular Theory.* Chicago: University of Chicago Press, 1984.

Baker, Houston A., Jr., and Patricia Redmond, eds. *Afro-American Literary Study in the 1990's.* Chicago: University of Chicago Press, 1989.

Bakhtin, Mikhail M. "Discourse in the Novel." In *Critical Theory since 1965,* ed. Hazard Adams and Leroy Searle, 665–78. Tallahassee: University of Florida Press, 1986.

Barrett, Lindon. *Blackness and Value: Seeing Double.* New York: Cambridge University Press, 1999.

Bassard, Katherine Clay. *Spiritual Interrogations: Culture, Gender, and Community in Early African American Women's Writing.* Princeton: Princeton University Press, 1999.

Bate, Walter Jackson. *The Burden of the Past and the English Poet.* Cambridge, MA: Belknap, 1970.

———. *John Keats.* Cambridge, MA: Belknap, 1963.

Benezet, Anthony. *Some Historical Account of Guinea, Its Situation, Produce, and the General Disposition of Its Inhabitants: with an Inquiry into the Rise and*

*Progress of the Slave Trade, Its Nature and Lamentable Effects.* 1771. Reprint, London: J. Phillips, 1788.

Blake, William. *The Complete Poetry and Prose.* Edited by David Erdman and Harold Bloom. New York: Anchor, 1988.

Boulukos, George E. "Maria Edgeworth's 'Grateful Negro' and the Sentimental Argument for Slavery." *Eighteenth-Century Life* 23, 1 (1999): 12–29.

Bové, Paul. "Discourse." In *Critical Terms for Literary Study*, ed. Frank Lentricchia and Thomas McLaughlin, 50–65. Chicago: University of Chicago Press, 1990.

———. "Foreword: The Foucault Phenomenon: The Problematics of Style." In *Foucault*, by Gilles Deleuze, vii–xl. Minneapolis: University of Minnesota Press, 1986.

Brody, Jennifer DeVere. *Impossible Purities: Blackness, Femininity, and Victorian Culture.* Durham, NC: Duke University Press, 1998.

Buell, Lawrence. *Literary Transcendentalism: Style and Vision in the American Renaissance.* Ithaca: Cornell University Press, 1973.

Burke, Edmund. *Reflections on the Revolution in France.* Edited by L. G. Mitchell. Oxford and New York: Oxford University Press, 1999.

Carlyle, Thomas. *Occasional Discourse on the Nigger Question.* London: T. Bosworth, 1853.

Carretta, Vincent. "Olaudah Equiano or Gustavus Vassa?: New Light on an Eighteenth-Century Question of Identity." *Slavery and Abolition* 20, 3 (1999): 96–105.

Chartier, Roger. "Texts, Printing, Readings." In *The New Cultural History*, ed. Lynn Hunt, 154–75. Berkeley: University of California Press, 1989.

Child, Lydia Maria. *An Appeal in Favor of That Class of Americans Called Africans.* Amherst: University of Massachusetts Press, 1996.

Clarkson, Thomas. *An Essay on the Slavery and Commerce of the Human Species, Particularly the African.* New York: AMS Press, 1972.

———. *The History of the Rise, Progress, and Accomplishment of the Abolition of the African Slave Trade by the British Parliament.* London: Longman, Hurst, Rees, and Orme, 1808.

Costanzo, Angelo. *Surprising Narrative: Olaudah Equiano and the Beginnings of Black Autobiography.* Westport, CT: Greenwood, 1987.

Cover, Robert M. *Justice Accused: Antislavery and the Judicial Process.* New Haven and London: Yale University Press, 1975.

Damrosch, Leopold. *Symbol and Truth in Blake's Myth.* Princeton: Princeton University Press, 1980.

Davis, Charles, and Henry Louis Gates, Jr., eds. *The Slave's Narrative.* Oxford and New York: Oxford University Press, 1985.

Davis, David Brion. *The Problem of Slavery in Western Culture*. Oxford and New York: Oxford University Press, 1966.

de Duras, Claire. *Ourika*. Edited by Roger Little. Exeter: University of Exeter Press, 1993.

————. *Ourika: An English Translation*. Translated by John Fowles. New York: Modern Language Association of America, 1994.

————. *Ourika: The Original French Text*. Edited by Joan DeJean. New York: Modern Language Association of America, 1994.

Delaney, Martin R. *Blake; or, The Huts of America* (1859–61). Edited by Floyd J. Miller. Boston: Beacon, 1970.

Deleuze, Gilles. *Foucault*. Minneapolis: University of Minnesota Press, 1986.

Douglass, Frederick. *Narrative of the Life of Frederick Douglass, An American Slave: Written by Himself*. Edited by David W. Blight. Boston: Bedford Books, 1993.

Dreyfus, Hubert L., and Paul Rabinow, eds. *Michel Foucault: Beyond Structuralism and Hermeneutics*. Chicago: University of Chicago Press, 1983.

Durant, Will. *The Story of Philosophy*. New York: Washington Square, 1961.

Dykes, Eva Beatrice. *The Negro in English Romantic Thought, or A Study of Sympathy for the Oppressed*. Washington, DC: Associated Publishers, 1942.

Earle, Thomas. *The Life, Travels and Opinions of Benjamin Lundy*. 1847. Reprint, New York: Augustus M. Kelley, 1971.

Emerson, Ralph Waldo. *Emerson's Antislavery Writings*. Edited by Len Gougeon and Joel Myerson. New Haven: Yale University Press, 1995.

————. *The Portable Emerson*. Edited by Carl Bode. New York: Penguin, 1981.

Equiano, Olaudah. *The Interesting Narrative of the Life of Olaudah Equiano, or Gustavus Vassa, the African. Written by Himself* (1789). In *The Classic Slave Narratives*, ed. Henry Louis Gates, Jr., 1–182. New York: Mentor, 1987.

Erkkila, Betsy. "Revolutionary Women." *Tulsa Studies in Women's Literature* 6, 2 (Fall 1987): 189–223.

————. "Phillis Wheatley and Black American Revolution." In *A Mixed Race: Ethnicity in Early America*, ed. Frank Sheffelton. Oxford and New York: Oxford University Press, 1993: 225–40.

*Extracts from the Evidence Taken before Committees of the Two Houses of Parliament Relative to the Slave Trade, with Illustrations from Collateral Sources*. 1851. Reprint, New York: Negro Universities Press, 1969.

*Extracts from the Evidence Taken before the Select Committee of the House of Commons*. Parliament of Great Britain. London: Strahan and Spottoswoode, 1818.

Faust, Drew Gilpin, ed. *The Ideology of Slavery: Proslavery Thought in the Antebellum South, 1830–1860*. Baton Rouge: Louisiana State University Press, 1981.

Favrod, Charles-Henri. *Étranges Étrangers: Photographie et exotisme, 1850/1910.* Paris: Centre Nationale de la Photographie, 1989.

Felman, Shoshana, and Dori Laub. *Testimony: Crises of Witnessing in Literature, Psychoanalysis, and History.* London and New York: Routledge, 1992.

Ferguson, Moira. *Subject to Others: British Women Writers and Colonial Slavery, 1670–1834.* London and New York: Routledge, 1992.

———. "Introduction." In *The History of Mary Prince: A West Indian Slave. Related by, Herself,* ed. Moira Ferguson, 1–41. 1987. Reprint, Ann Arbor: University of Michigan Press, 1993.

Fichtelberg, Joseph. "Words between Worlds: The Economy of Equiano's Narrative." *American Literary History* 5 (1993): 459–80.

Flanzbaum, Hilene. "Unprecedented Liberties: Re-reading Phillis Wheatley." *MELUS* 18, 3 (Fall 1993): 71–81.

Foster, Frances Smith. *Witnessing Slavery: The Development of Ante-Bellum Slave Narratives.* Westport, CT: Greenwood, 1979.

Foucault, Michel. *The Archeology of Knowledge.* Translated by Alan Sheridan. 1969. Reprint, New York: Pantheon, 1972.

———. *Discipline and Punish: The Birth of the Prison.* Translated by Alan Sheridan. 1975. Reprint, New York: Vintage, 1979.

———. "The Discourse on Language." In *The Archeology of Knowledge,* trans. Alan Sheridan. 1969. Reprint, New York: Pantheon, 1972: 215–37.

———. *The Order of Things: An Archeology of the Human Sciences.* 1966. Reprint, New York: Vintage, 1973.

Franklin, John Hope. *From Slavery to Freedom.* New York: Knopf, 1964.

Fuller, Margaret. *The Portable Margaret Fuller.* Edited by Mary Kelley. New York: Penguin, 1994.

Gates, Henry Louis, Jr. *Figures in Black: Words, Signs and the "Racial" Self.* Oxford and New York: Oxford University Press, 1987.

———, ed. *The Classic Slave Narratives.* New York: Mentor, 1987.

———, ed. *"Race," Writing and Difference.* Chicago: University of Chicago Press, 1985.

Gaull, Marilyn. *English Romanticism: The Human Context.* New York and London: Norton, 1988.

Gerzina, Gretchen. *Black London: Life before Emancipation.* New Brunswick, NJ: Rutgers University Press, 1995.

Gilroy, Paul. *The Black Atlantic: Modernity and Double Consciousness.* Cambridge, MA: Harvard University Press, 1993.

Gossett, Thomas. *Race: The History of an Idea in America.* New York: Schocken, 1965.

Gross, Seymour. *Images of the Negro in American Literature.* Chicago: University of Chicago Press, 1966.

Harris, Middleton. *The Black Book.* New York: Random House, 1974.

Hartman, Saidya V. *Scenes of Subjection: Terror, Slavery, and Self-Making in Nineteenth-Century America.* Oxford and New York: Oxford University Press, 1997.

Haskell, Thomas. "Capitalism and the Origins of the Humanitarian Sensibility, Part 1." *American Historical Review* 90, 2 (April 1985): 339–61.

———. "Capitalism and the Origins of the Humanitarian Sensibility, Part 2." *American Historical Review* 90, 3 (June 1985): 547–66.

Hegel, G. W. F. *The Philosophy of History.* New York: Dover, 1956.

Heidegger, Martin. "The Origin of the Work of Art." In *Poetry, Language, Thought,* 15–87. New York: Harper & Row, 1971.

Higman, Barry W. *Slave Populations of the British Caribbean, 1807–1834.* Baltimore: Johns Hopkins University Press, 1984.

Hobbes, Thomas. *Leviathan.* Edited by C. B. Macpherson. Baltimore: Penguin, 1968.

Jacobs, Harriet. *Incidents in the Life of a Slave Girl* (1861). Edited by Jean Fegan Yellin. Cambridge, MA, and London: Harvard University Press, 1987.

James, William Lloyd. "The Black Man in English Romantic Literature, 1772–1833." Ph.D. Diss., University of California, Los Angeles, 1977.

Jefferson, Thomas. *Notes on the State of Virginia.* Edited by William Peden. Chapel Hill: University of North Carolina Press, 1955.

Johnson, Paul. *A History of the American People.* New York: HarperCollins, 1997.

Jordan, June. "The Difficult Miracle of Black Poetry in America." *Massachusetts Review* (Summer 1986): 252–62.

Jordan, Winthrop D. *White over Black: American Attitudes toward the Negroes, 1550–1812.* Chapel Hill: University of North Carolina Press, 1968.

Kelley, Robin D. G., and Earl Lewis, eds. *To Make Our World Anew: A History of African Americans.* New York: Oxford University Press, 2000.

Levernier, James A. "Phillis Wheatley." *Legacy* 13, 1 (1996): 64–75.

———. "Phillis Wheatley and the New England Clergy." *Early American Literature* 26, 1 (1991): 21–38.

———. "Style as Protest in the Poetry of Phillis Wheatley." *Style* 27, 2 (Summer 1993): 172–93.

Littlefield, Daniel C. "Revolutionary Citizens: 1776–1804." In *To Make Our World Anew: A History of African Americans,* ed. Robin D. G. Kelley and Earl Lewis. Oxford and New York: Oxford University Press, 2000: 103–68.

Locke, John. *An Essay concerning Human Understanding.* Edited by Roger Woolhouse. New York: Penguin, 1997.

Marx, Karl. *The Grundrisse.* Edited and translated by David McLellen. New York: Harper & Row, 1971.

Mathieson, William Law. *British Slavery and Its Abolition, 1823–1838.* New York: Octagon, 1967.

McBride, Dwight A. "Speaking the Unspeakable: On Toni Morrison, African American Intellectuals and the Uses of Essentialist Rhetoric." In *Reading Toni Morrison: Theoretical and Critical Approaches,* ed. Nancy J. Peterson, 131–52. Baltimore: Johns Hopkins University Press, 1997.

McFarland, Thomas. *Romantic Cruxes: The English Essayists and the Spirit of the Age.* Oxford and New York: Oxford University Press, 1987.

———. *Romanticism and the Forms of Ruin: Wordsworth, Coleridge, and Modalities of Fragmentation.* Princeton: Princeton University Press, 1981.

McGann, Jerome J., ed. *The Oxford Book of Romantic Period Verse.* Oxford and New York: Oxford University Press, 1993.

———. *The Poetics of Sensibility: A Revolution in Literary Style.* New York: Clarendon, 1996.

McGary, Howard, and Bill E. Lawson. *Between Slavery and Freedom: Philosophy and American Slavery.* Bloomington: Indiana University Press, 1992.

McKay, Claude. "If We Must Die." In *The Heath Anthology of American Literature,* vol. 2, ed. Paul Lauter, 1691. Lexington: Heath, 1994.

Meier, August. *Negro Thought in America, 1880–1915.* Ann Arbor: University of Michigan Press, 1964.

Mellor, Anne. *Romanticism and Gender.* London and New York: Routledge, 1993.

Mellor, Anne K., and Richard E. Matlak, eds. *British Literature, 1780–1830.* Fort Worth: Harcourt Brace Jovanovich, 1996.

Midgley, Clare. *Women against Slavery: The British Campaigns, 1780–1870.* London and New York: Routledge, 1992.

Montesquieu. *The Spirit of the Laws.* Translated and edited by Anne M. Cohler, Basia Carolyn Miller, and Harold Samuel Stone. Cambridge: Cambridge University Press, 1989.

Morrison, Toni. *Beloved.* New York: Knopf, 1987.

———. *Playing in the Dark: Whiteness and the Literary Imagination.* New York: Vintage, 1993.

Nelson, Truman, ed. *Documents of Upheaval: Selections from William Lloyd Garrison's* The Liberator, *1831–1865.* New York: Hill and Wang, 1966.

Newey, Vincent. "The Abolition of the Slave Trade." In *A Handbook to British Romanticism,* ed. Jean Raimond and J. R. Watson. New York: St. Martin's, 1992: 1–4.

Nietzsche, Friedrich. *Beyond Good and Evil: Prelude to a Philosophy of the Future.* Edited and translated by Walter Kaufmann. New York: Vintage, 1989.

———. *The Birth of Tragedy*. Oxford: Oxford University Press, 2000.

———. "On Truth and Lie in an Extra Moral Sense." In *The Portable Nietzsche*, trans. and ed. Walter Kaufmann, 42–47. New York: Penguin, 1982.

Nott, Walt. "From 'Uncultivated Barbarian' to 'Poetical Genius': The Public Presence of Phillis Wheatley." *MELUS* 18, 3 (Fall 1993): 21–32.

Olney, James. "'I Was Born': Slave Narratives, Their Status as Autobiography and as Literature." In *The Slave's Narrative*, ed. Charles Davis and Henry Louis Gates, Jr. Oxford and New York: Oxford University Press, 1985: 148–74.

Orban, Katalin. "Dominant and Submerged Discourses in *The Life of Olaudah Equiano* (or Gustavus Vassa?)." *African American Review* 27, 4 (Winter 1993): 655–64.

Paine, Thomas. *The Complete Writings of Thomas Paine*. Edited by Philip S. Foner. New York: Citadel, 1945.

Perkins, David. *English Romantic Writers*. New York: Harcourt, Brace & World, 1967.

Pieterse, Jan Nederveen. *White on Black: Images of Africa and Blacks in Western Popular Culture*. New Haven and London: Yale University Press, 1992.

Prince, Mary. *The History of Mary Prince: A West Indian Slave. Related by Herself* (1831). Edited by Moira Ferguson. Ann Arbor: University of Michigan Press, 1993.

Quarles, Benjamin. *Black Abolitionists*. New York: Da Capo, 1969.

Raboteau, Albert J. *Slave Religion: The "Invisible Institution" in the Antebellum South*. New York: Oxford University Press, 1978.

Raimond, Jean, and J. R. Watson, eds. *A Handbook to British Romanticism*. New York: St. Martin's, 1992.

Redding, J. Saunders. *To Make a Poet Black*. New York: Core Collection, 1939.

Reid-Pharr, Robert. *Conjugal Union: The Body, the House and the Black American*. Oxford and New York: Oxford University Press, 1999.

Reising, Russell J. *Loose Ends: Closure and Crisis in the American Social Text*. Durham, NC: Duke University Press, 1996.

Rice, C. Duncan. *The Rise and Fall of Black Slavery*. New York: Harper & Row, 1975.

Richardson, Alan, and Sonia Hofkosh, eds. *Romanticism, Race, and Imperial Culture, 1780–1834*. Bloomington: Indiana University Press, 1996.

Roach, Joseph R. "Slave Spectacles and Tragic Octoroons: A Cultural Genealogy of Antebellum Performance." *Theatre Survey* 33, 2 (November 1992): 167–87.

Robinson, William H. *Phillis Wheatley in the Black American Beginnings*. Detroit: Broadside, 1975.

———, ed. *Critical Essays on Phillis Wheatley*. Boston: Hall, 1982.

Rodriguez, Junius P., ed. *The Historical Encyclopedia of World Slavery, Volume One.* Santa Barbara: ABC-CLIO, 1997.

Roof, Judith, and Robyn Wiegman, eds. *Who Can Speak? Authority and Critical Identity.* Urbana and Chicago: University of Illinois Press, 1995.

Rousseau, Jean-Jacques. *The Essential Rousseau.* Translated by Lowell Bair. New York: Meridian, 1975.

Sala-Molins, Louis. *Le Code Noir: Ou le calvaire de Canaan.* Paris: Presses Universitaires de France, 1987.

Samuels, Wilfred D. "Disguised Voice in *The Interesting Narrative of Olaudah Equiano, or Gustavus Vassa, the African.*" *Black American Literature Forum* 19 (1985): 64–69.

Sandiford, Keith A. *Measuring the Moment: Strategies of Protest in Eighteenth-Century Afro-English Writing.* Selinsgrove, PA: Susquehanna University Press, 1988.

Scott, George. *The History of Torture.* London: Senate, 1995.

Scott, James C. *Domination and the Arts of Resistance: Hidden Transcripts.* New Haven and London: Yale University Press, 1990.

Sekora, John, and Darwin T. Turner, eds. *The Art of the Slave Narrative.* Macomb: Western Illinois University Press, 1982.

Sharpe, Jenny. "'Something Akin to Freedom': The Case of Mary Prince" 8.1 (1996): 31–55.

Shepherd, David. "Bakhtin and the Reader." In *Bakhtin and Cultural Theory,* ed. Ken Hirschkop and David Shepherd, 91–108. Manchester and New York: Manchester University Press, 1989.

Simons, Jon. *Foucault and the Political.* London and New York: Routledge, 1995.

Smith, Valerie. *Self-Discovery and Authority in Afro-American Narrative.* Cambridge, MA: Harvard University Press, 1987.

Spivak, Gayatri. "Can the Subaltern Speak?" In *Marxism and the Interpretation of Culture,* ed. Cary Nelson and Lawrence Grossberg, 271–313. Urbana and Chicago: University of Illinois Press, 1988.

———. *The Post-Colonial Critic.* London and New York: Routledge, 1990.

Starling, Marion Wilson. *The Slave Narrative: Its Place in American History.* Boston: G. K. Hall, 1982.

Stephen, George. *Antislavery Recollections: In a Series of Letters Addressed to Mrs. Beecher Stowe, Written by Sir George Stephen, at Her Request.* London: Thomas Hatchard, 1854.

Stepto, Robert. "Narration, Authentication, and Authorial Control in Frederick Douglass' Narrative of 1845." In *African American Autobiography: A Collection of Critical Essays,* ed. William L. Andrews. Englewood Cliffs, NJ: Prentice-Hall, 1993: 26–35.

Stowe, Harriet Beecher. *Uncle Tom's Cabin, or, Life among the Lowly.* New York: Penguin, 1986.

Stuckey, Sterling. *Slave Culture: Nationalist Theory and the Foundations of Black America.* Oxford and New York: Oxford University Press, 1987.

Sundquist, Eric J. *To Wake the Nations: Race in the Making of American Literature.* Cambridge, MA: Belknap, 1993.

Taylor, Charles. *The Ethics of Authenticity.* Cambridge, MA: Harvard University Press, 1991.

———. "Foucault on Freedom and Truth." In *Foucault: A Critical Reader,* ed. David Couzens Hoy, 69–102. Oxford and Cambridge: Blackwell, 1986.

Temperley, Howard. *British Antislavery, 1833–1870.* Columbia: University of South Carolina Press, 1972.

Thomas, Helen. *Romanticism and Slave Narratives: Transatlantic Testimonies.* Cambridge: Cambridge University Press, 2000.

Turner, Lorenzo D. *Anti-Slavery Sentiment in American Literature prior to 1865.* Port Washington: Kennikat, 1966.

Walker, David. *David Walker's Appeal to the Colored Citizens of the World, but in Particular, and Very Expressly, to Those of the United States of America.* Baltimore: Black Classic Press, 1993.

West, Cornel. *Race Matters.* Boston: Beacon, 1993.

Wheatley, Phillis. *The Collected Works of Phillis Wheatley.* Edited by John Shields. Oxford and New York: Oxford University Press, 1988.

Williams, Eric. *Capitalism and Slavery.* New York: G. P. Putnam, 1966.

Williams, Patricia J. *The Alchemy of Race and Rights.* Cambridge, MA: Harvard University Press, 1991.

Wilson, Harriet. *Our Nig, or Sketches from the Life of a Free Black, in a Two-Story White House, North, Showing That Slavery's Shadows Fall Even There.* 1859. Reprint, New York: Vintage, 1983.

Winthrop, John. "A Modell of Christian Charity." In *The Heath Anthology of American Literature,* vol. 2, ed. Paul Lauter. Lexington: Heath, 1994: 226–34.

Wollstonecraft, Mary. *A Vindication of the Rights of Man.* Amherst, NY: Prometheus Books, 1996.

———. *A Vindication of the Rights of Woman.* New York: Penguin, 1985.

Woolman, John. *Some Considerations on the Keeping of Negroes.* In *The Heath Anthology of American Literature,* vol. 2, ed. Paul Lauter. Lexington: Heath, 1994: 621–27.

# INDEX

Abolition, 1–8, 13–25, 27–34, 40–50, 54,
  56, 62–65, 69, 71, 75, 76, 78–83, 88,
  92, 93, 103, 104, 111, 112, 116, 124,
  135, 146, 153, 157, 158, 161–163, 167,
  168, 172, 174, 175
Affirmative action, 173, 174
Africa, 1, 8, 24, 26, 30, 35, 113, 114, 117,
  121, 124, 125, 129, 130
African American, 15, 72, 76, 92, 111, 122,
  140, 158, 172
Afro-American, 87
Agency Committee, 39
Allison, Robert J., 26, 27, 125–127
Ameliorationist, 50, 51
America, 17, 18, 20, 21, 29, 30, 63–65, 67,
  68, 79, 80, 83, 84, 104, 106, 109, 113,
  114, 118, 141, 153, 154, 157, 162
Anderson, Benedict, 151
Andrews, William L., 86–88
Antebellum, 154
Anti-slavery, 1, 2, 30, 32, 33, 40, 63–65, 89,
  100, 148, 150
*Anti-Slavery Monthly Reporter*, 36
Anti-Slavery Society
  Society for the Mitigation and Gradual
    Abolition of Slavery throughout the
    British Dominions, 18, 37, 38, 39,
    95–96
Apter, Emily, 91
Augustan Age, 42
Authentic, 4–6, 25, 81, 85, 89, 95, 96,
  98, 99, 128, 134, 136, 140, 145, 158,
  164
Autobiography, 9, 23, 87, 97, 121

Bailyn, Bernard, 68
Baker, Houston A., Jr., 121–124
Bakhtin, Mikhail, 15, 152
Barrett, Lindon, 91
Bear witness, 4, 8, 15, 16, 91, 94, 95, 142,
  156, 171
*Beloved*, 11, 12, 65
Benezet, Anthony, 30, 129, 130, 147
Black, 4, 5, 8, 11, 13, 15–17, 21, 23, 25, 26,
  31, 43, 45, 47, 54–57, 60–62, 76,
  78–81, 83, 87, 92, 93, 95, 98, 101, 103,

105, 107, 109–114, 116, 123, 132, 133,
  136, 137, 140, 141, 151, 158, 164
Black women, 11, 23, 87
Blake, William, 8, 59, 61, 170
Blight, David W., 157, 158, 162, 163
Body, 4, 5, 8, 11, 61, 62, 80, 81, 83, 98
Burke, Edmund, 20, 21
Buxton, 37, 38

Carlyle, Thomas, 24, 34, 59
Chinssole, 125
Christianity, 2, 13, 14, 45, 57, 58, 60, 62,
  68, 103, 105, 109, 112–114, 116, 118,
  120, 125, 128, 142, 150, 151, 168, 170,
  171, 173
Clarkson, Thomas, 27, 30, 37, 94
Climatology, 1, 132
Collective
  black body, 11, 83
  slave body, 10
Committee on the Slave Trade, 29
Community, 11, 12, 29, 71, 72, 85, 86,
  101, 102, 109, 148, 151, 163, 164, 170,
  174
Compromise of 1877, 66
Construction, 2, 8, 9, 51, 56, 60, 77, 140,
  158
Context, 1, 2, 4–6, 11, 12, 17, 18, 24, 42,
  53, 71, 72, 74, 77–79, 86, 101, 103–
  105, 110, 111, 118, 122, 142, 148, 152,
  153, 156, 162, 172
Convention, 14, 128
Costanzo, Angelo, 121, 125, 129, 130
Cowper, William, 42, 43, 54, 57, 58
Cross-cultural, 22, 23
Cugano, Ottobah, 126, 127

Damrosch, Leo, 61
Dartmouth, Earl of, 118
Davis, Charles T., 24, 42, 68, 69, 73
Day, Thomas, 142
Deane, Charles, 65
Democrat, 70, 73
Dickens, Charles, 24
Discourse, 1–8, 12, 13, 15, 16, 40, 80, 89,
  92, 116, 119, 122, 123, 128, 131, 143,

Discourse *(continued)*
    148, 151, 152, 154, 156–162, 164–166,
    169–172, 174, 175
  discursive concerns, 7, 123, 151
  discursive reader, 15, 151, 152, 154,
    156, 158, 159–162, 164, 165, 166, 169,
    170–172, 175
  discursive regularities, 3
  discursive terrain, 3–6, 8, 13, 16, 128,
    151, 158, 174
Douglass, Frederick, 14, 15, 40, 62, 75–77,
    80, 95, 151–172
Durant, Will, 139
Duras, Claire,
Dykes, Eva Beatrice, 24

Edgeworth, Maria, 42–48, 50, 52–54, 58,
    87, 162, 169
1808 Slave Trade Act, 63
Emerson, Ralph Waldo, 7, 17, 63, 67–69,
    70–74, 77, 154
Equiano, Olaudah, 14, 26, 27, 54, 93, 96,
    103, 120–150, 158, 166
Exorcism, 11
Experience
  epistemology of, 13
Ex-slave, 5, 97

Felman, Shoshana, 141
Ferguson, Moira, 42, 67, 85, 86, 88
Fichtelberg, Joseph, 122, 124
Foucault, Michel, 4–7, 122
Fowles, John, 24
Fox-Grenville Ministry, 34
Franklin, Benjamin, 20
Franklin, John Hope, 66
French Revolution, 20, 22
Fugitive Slave Act, 65
Fuller, Margaret, 8, 75–78, 80, 95, 154

Garner, Margaret, 65
Garrison, William Lloyd, 6, 18, 64, 78–81,
    83, 162, 163
  abolition, 64
Gates, Henry Louis Jr., 17, 24, 72, 75,
    86–88, 104, 107, 123
Genre, 2, 3, 14, 23, 158, 172
Gilroy, Paul, 23
Gothic, 10, 21

Half-Way Covenant, 135
Hammon, Jupiter, 110, 111
Hartely, David, 29
Hartman, Saidya, 154, 156, 160
Hayes, Rutherford B., 66
Hegel, George W. Friedrich, 1, 8, 19, 108
  master-slave dialectic, 13, 18, 47
Hegemony, 13, 25, 46, 66, 92
Higman, Barry W., 36
*History of Mary Prince, The: A West Indian
    Slave. Related by Herself,* 8, 13, 24, 85,
    86, 88, 93, 94, 98, 100, 108, 141
Holocaust, 139, 141
Hopkins, Samuel, 117
Horton, George Moses, 110–112
House of Commons, 34, 36
House of Lords, 34
Humboldt, Alexander von, 24
Hume, David, 107, 108

Identity, 12, 21, 25, 73, 100, 113, 140, 141,
    148

Jackson, Jesse, 77
Jacobs, Harriet, 93, 94, 96, 154
Jefferson, Thomas, 7, 18, 20, 123, 131–
    133, 135, 136, 147
Jim Crow laws,
Johnson, Barbara, 71
Johnson, Paul, 29
Jordan, June, 112
Jordan, Winthrop, 63

Kant, Immanuel, 107
Kipling, Rudyard, 46
Knipe, Eliza, 43

Laub, Dori, 141
Liberation, 15, 28, 79, 104, 114, 116, 123
*Liberator, The,* 64, 78, 79
*Lieux de memoire,* 9
Littlefield, Daniel, 29
London Abolition Committee, 29
Long, Edward, 24
Lundy, Benjamin, 79–83

Malcolm X (Masjid El Hajj Malik El
    Shabazz), 144
Mansfield, Lord, 25, 27

Manumission, 37, 86, 123, 124
Marx, Karl, 91
  Marxist, 124
Master, 2, 9, 13, 17–19, 25, 41, 44, 45, 47,
  48, 50, 53, 62, 74, 88, 95, 101, 103,
  109, 117, 135, 137, 138, 145, 146,
  167–169, 171
Meeting for Sufferings, 29, 30
Meier, August, 66
Mellor, Anne K., 22, 45, 46
Memory, 8–10, 26, 94, 97
Metaphor, 10, 141
  of theater, 8
  metaphorical landmarks, 10
Midgley, Clare, 42
Milton, John, 106, 147
Montesquieu, 2, 18–20, 123
Morrison, Toni, 11, 65

Narrative, 3, 6, 7, 9–14, 16, 17, 25, 43, 47,
  49, 51, 54, 85, 86, 88, 90, 91, 93–100,
  120–129, 135, 136, 138, 139–142, 145,
  147–150, 153–157, 160, 161, 164–167,
  170–172
  narrating, 157
  narration, 9, 12, 86, 87, 90, 97, 133, 139,
    163, 164
  narrator, 3, 4, 10, 11, 48–51, 86, 87, 89,
    94, 121, 123, 124, 135, 140, 142, 145,
    148, 150, 159, 163, 164
Narrative of the Life of Frederick Douglass, An
  American Slave: Written by Himself, 14,
  75, 150–159, 161, 164, 165, 167,
  170–172
Native American, 118, 133
Natural law discourse, 13, 18, 68
Natural rights discourse, 13–15, 18–20,
  92, 103, 107, 148, 149, 151, 158
Nature, 2, 6–9, 14, 17, 22, 24, 26, 46, 52, 55,
  70, 73, 77, 82, 91, 114, 129, 131, 132,
  134, 141, 142, 145, 147, 149, 157, 165
Negro, 7, 20, 30, 36, 43, 46–48, 54–59, 66,
  81, 87, 98, 104, 110, 111, 113, 117,
  130, 137, 145, 146
Nelson, Truman, 78, 81
Nietzsche, Friedrich, 7, 19, 139, 142
Notes on the State of Virginia, 7, 18, 123, 131,
  136
Nott, Walt, 105

Olney, James, 9, 96
Opie, Amelia A., 43
Orban, Katalin, 123
Other, 47, 61, 91, 92, 136
  Otherness, 60, 61, 136

Paine, Thomas, 18, 20, 21
Penn, William, 30
Pieterse, Jan Nederveen, 24
Poetry, 14, 42, 62, 65, 103, 104, 106, 108,
  110, 112, 113, 119, 133
  poetic language, 14, 22, 103
Politics, 2, 5, 7, 8, 13–15, 18, 19, 21–23,
  25, 26, 28, 29, 32, 33, 34, 39–42, 46,
  47, 53, 59, 65, 66, 69, 72, 81–83, 86,
  89, 90, 95, 96, 105, 108, 113, 114, 116,
  117, 119, 120, 123, 124, 128, 132, 143,
  144, 148, 151, 157, 162, 172–174
Pope, Alexander, 106
Prince, Mary, 9–11, 13, 77, 85–96, 98–102,
  156, 161
Pringle, Thomas, 95, 96, 98, 99
Pro-slavery, 2, 8, 14–16, 24, 25, 43, 54, 59,
  60, 62, 71, 77, 79, 80, 86, 87, 92, 95,
  103, 148, 149, 151, 158, 160, 164–166,
  170, 171
Proust, Marcel, 97
Providence, 127, 166
Puritan, 63, 135

Quakers, 29–31, 63, 130

Race, 2, 111, 45, 53, 56, 60, 67, 75, 76, 83,
  95, 104, 107, 111, 113, 114, 116, 132
  racial, 2, 15, 21, 46, 56, 60, 61, 67, 73,
    74, 77, 84, 103, 110, 114, 117, 143
  racial subjugation, 15
  racialized discourse, 17, 18, 21, 52, 60,
    63, 75
  racist, 8, 17, 24, 62, 67, 109, 119
Ramsey, James, 27
Reader, 2, 3, 6, 14, 15, 22, 40, 45, 47, 49,
  50, 56, 59, 69, 87, 89, 90, 92, 94, 96,
  99, 106, 113, 114, 118, 120, 121, 123,
  126, 127, 132, 134, 135, 136, 142,
  151–156, 158–161, 163, 165, 166, 168,
  169, 171
  readership, 7, 89, 115, 118, 125, 130,
    156

Reconstruction, 66
Redding, J. Saunders, 104, 110–112
Reform Bill, 41
Reid-Pharr, Robert, 105
Religious rhetoric, 13, 14, 40, 83, 103, 125
Representation, 11, 13, 16, 21–23, 43, 84,
    86, 89, 96, 101, 113, 113, 139, 148,
    159, 162, 169, 170
  representational politics, 12, 54, 140
Rhetoric, 1, 2, 3, 6, 8, 11, 13, 15, 16, 18,
    32–34, 40, 51, 53, 54, 59, 60, 61, 69,
    71, 72, 74–78, 80–83, 89, 92–95, 98,
    101–103, 114, 116, 117, 119, 124, 125,
    131–136, 145, 148, 152, 153, 157, 158,
    161, 162, 166, 167, 173, 174
  rhetorical peerformativity, 6
  rhetorical strategies, 3, 11, 16, 103, 152,
    158, 174
  of whiteness, 8
Rice, C. Duncan, 31
Robinson, William H., 65, 104, 111
Rogers, Nathaniel P., 157
Romantic, 6, 17, 21–23, 42, 141, 154, 160
Romanticism, 13, 17, 18, 21–23, 45
Romantics, 6, 22
Rousseau, Jean Jacques, 18–20, 142, 143,
    146, 149
Russwurm, John, 111

Samuels, Wilfred D., 125
Sancho, Ignatius, 133
Sandiford, Keith, 121
Segregation, 66
Sellman, James Clyde, 30
Shakespeare, William, 44, 97
Sharp, Granville, 25, 27, 30
Sharpe, Jenny, 77
Shields, John C., 116
Signification, 8, 62, 140
Slave, 2–19, 21, 23–25, 27–29, 32–37,
    41–43, 45, 47, 50, 52–59, 63, 65, 69,
    74, 75, 79, 81, 84–98, 100–102, 105,
    109, 110, 113, 116, 119, 121–125, 130,
    135–140, 142–175
  auction, 4
Slave narrator, 2, 3, 4, 16, 97, 139, 151,
    156
Slave witness, 2, 6, 8, 113, 151, 152, 156,
    157, 163, 164, 166, 174, 175

Slavery, 1–4, 6–34, 39, 40, 43, 47, 50, 52,
    54–56, 58, 59, 62–65, 68, 69, 71, 73,
    74, 76–79, 83–85, 86–98, 100–105,
    108, 114–116, 120–127, 129–131,
    134–136, 139–143, 145, 146, 149–169,
    171, 174, 175
Smith, Valerie, 125
Society for the Abolition of Slave Trade,
    18, 31, 35
Somerset, James, 25
Somerset case (1772), 25–27
Songs of Innocence, 59
Spectacle, 139, 160
Stephen, George, 39, 82
Stowe, Harriet Beecher, 39, 62, 65, 82, 154
Subjectivity, 14, 47, 69, 72, 73

Tabula rasa, 50, 142
Tanner, Obour, 118
Testimony, 2, 5–7, 9, 10, 13–15, 36, 90, 91,
    94–96, 99, 100, 101, 113, 120, 124,
    126, 128, 130, 135, 142, 145, 146, 151,
    153–157, 161, 163, 166, 171, 172
  testimonial moments, 103
  Testimony: Crises of Witnessing in Litera-
    ture, Psychoanalysis, and History, 141
  slave, 2, 10, 14, 15, 25, 42, 101, 139, 151,
    154, 157, 158, 162, 165, 166, 172–175
Thackeray, William Makepeace, 24
Theatrical, 6, 116
Theatricality, 6
Torture, 10, 11, 54, 55, 139, 147
Transatlantic, 4, 14, 21, 23
Trollope, Anthony, 24
Turner, Lorenzo, D., 63

Uncle Tom's Cabin, 62, 65, 154

Walker, David, 6, 7, 78–83, 120
Webster, Daniel, 74
West, Cornel, 142
Wheatley, John, 105
Wheatley, Phillis, 13, 14, 65, 93, 103–106,
    108–120, 125, 133, 135
  "On Being Brought from Africa to
    America," 113
  "On Messrs. Hussey and Coffin," 106
  "On the Death of General Wooster,"
    116

"On the Death of the Rev. Mr. George Whitefield," 106, 116

"To the University of Cambridge in New England," 112

Whig, 70, 73

Whiteness, 59, 67, 77

White subjectivity, 46, 54, 55

Wilberforce, William, 30

Williams, Eric, 31

Witness, 2, 4–6, 8–11, 15, 16, 42, 75, 85, 89–91, 94–96, 98–100, 102, 103, 116, 136, 139, 142, 143, 145, 151–157, 159–161, 171, 175

Wollestonecraft, Mary, 21, 23, 162

Woman, 14, 22, 23, 31, 37, 42–46, 86, 87, 99, 107, 110, 119, 131, 137, 160, 162, 169, 173

Woolman, John, 30

Zong case (1781), 25, 26, 27

# ABOUT THE AUTHOR

Dwight A. McBride is head of the Department of African-American Studies and associate professor of English and African-American Studies at the University of Illinois at Chicago. He is editor of *James Baldwin Now,* also available from NYU Press, and coeditor of a special issue of *Callaloo* titled "Plum Nelly: New Essays in Black Queer Studies" (Winter 2000), both of which received special citation from the Crompton-Noll Award Committee of the Modern Language Association for their significant contribution to LGBT Studies.